For
Father
from
Evelyn
Christmas 1952

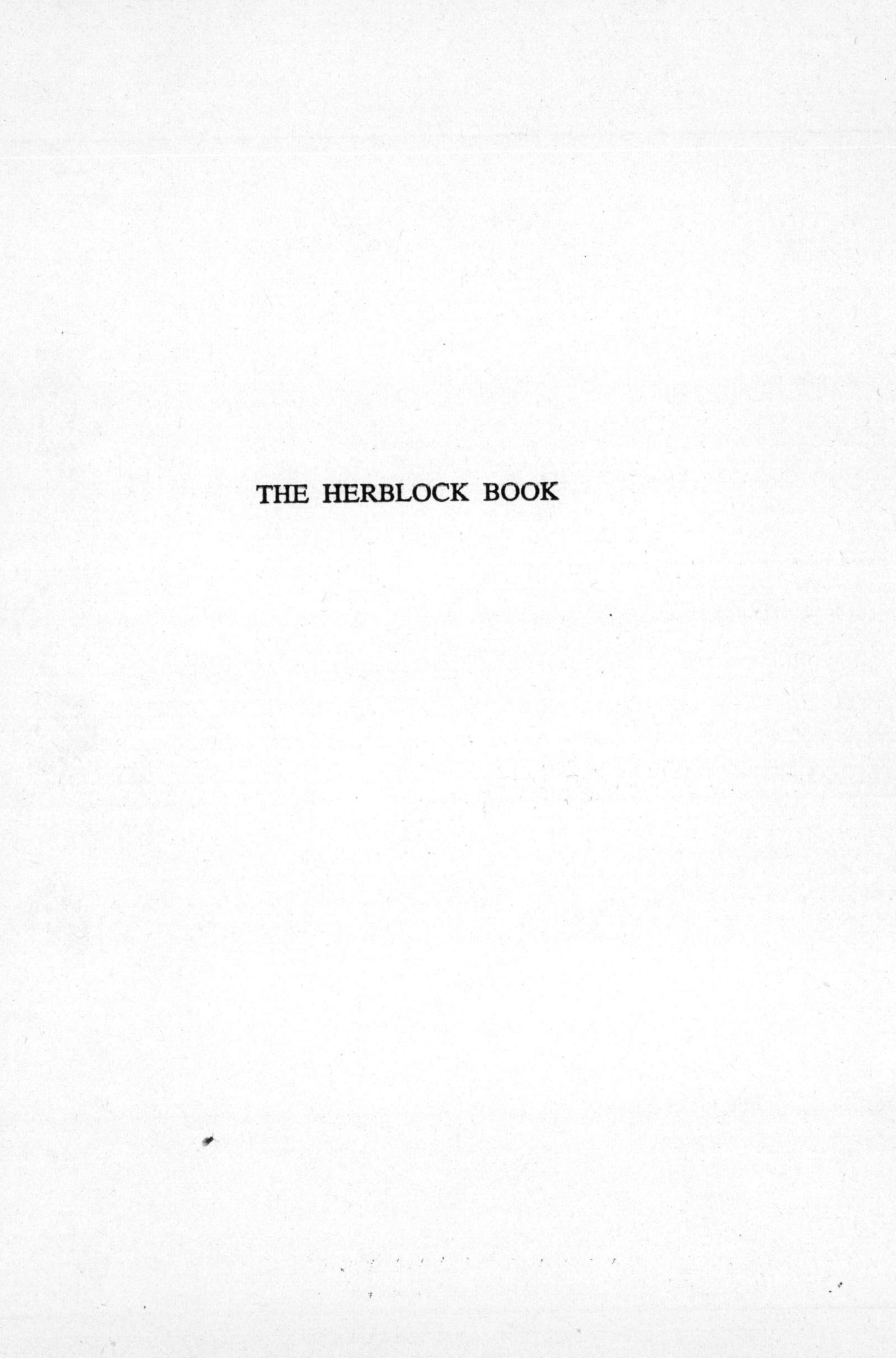

THE HERBLOCK BOOK

THE HERBLOCK BOOK

Text and Cartoons by

Herbert Block

THE BEACON PRESS · BOSTON

Most of the cartoons in this book appeared originally in the Washington *Post* and were distributed by the Post-Hall Syndicate (New York).

Printed in U. S. A.

FOR

TESSIE BLOCK

Contents

THE HERBLOCK BOOK

I

Begin Here

I'D HARDLY BE GIVING AWAY any trade secrets if I told you how a book like this comes to be written, because I'm not really in the trade. In this particular author-reader relationship—if it can be called that—we're both starting from scratch.

Briefly, the production of an amateur writing job like this is divided into two periods. The first—or "getting started"—phase is inclined to be somewhat difficult. But this period is soon over, and for the rest of the way you are in the second—or "completing the job"—phase, which is simply a living hell.

The only other hot information I can offer is that this introduction is done last, so that I can tell you what you're in for if you go any farther.

What you seem to have got hold of here is a kind of free-wheeling book of commentary. It's not a complete history of political events, not a definitive work on any subject, and it's not "inside" anything except my head. The cartoons are about things that have been of interest to me these last few years that I think are pertinent today.

While you look at the pictures I run along on this sound track telling you how I feel about some of the subjects in general, recalling a few incidents here and there, and digressing every once in a while to mention something about the cartoons themselves.

It's like looking over somebody's album or portfolio while he rambles on making random observations—except that there are certain advantages to doing it this way. You don't need to say, "Oh," "Really!" or "You think so?" every ten seconds. And you can close the covers, shut me up, and knock off whenever you feel like it.

2

That Congress

Even a quick flip through the cartoons in this section will reveal that they are not entirely flattering to their subjects. As a matter of fact, many of them are somewhat on the critical side. And let's face it, that's the way they are *most* of the time. Every once in a while when a congressman or an entire session of Congress is on the pan, somebody is sure to say, "But they work so hard!" or "You don't know how hard they *work!*"

I *do* know how hard they work and I wish some of them would stop it.

The congressman's lot is not a happy one. And I have a special sympathy for them because their jobs probably involve more spare-time chores than mine. Just working here in Washington, even without having any constituents, you get a good number of visiting firemen. They come on business, or to see where their taxes are going, or to find out if it's true that this is a madhouse, or just because the travel agent couldn't think of any other place at the moment. And somebody always wants you to do something here, look up something there, or show somebody around somewhere else. Nice, friendly people, every one of them, and when you put them all together they spell murder.

Well, the congressmen have a lot more visitors to see and countless requests to fill; and they have to do all these things. Oh, they don't *have* to— just those who want to keep getting elected to office. That is, roughly—in round numbers—say about 99 per cent.

Then there's the correspondence that has to be taken care of. *Dear Congressman: What are you going to do about these moths around here, they're getting fierce.*

And—

I see in a book that everybody takes dope down there. Cut that out.

And—

Am forwarding my six-year-old boy postpaid to see Our Nation's Capitol. P.S.: He bites.

And—

Dear Sir: Fellow on the radio says to write your congressman so just thought I'd drop you a line. Yours truly.

All that stuff has to be answered.

I'm one of those people who can't change a typewriter ribbon without seeming to be doing a charade of the Laocoön group; and when I sit down to write a few letters, the stationery, envelopes, stamps, and things never seem to get co-ordinated. The fountain pen or something is always missing, and as soon as I turn my back to find it, the letters dart off and burrow into old newspapers. Generally I figure I'm coming out good if I lose only a few small-

"Rover, Have You Put Your Muzzle On Yet?"

Jan 48

denomination stamps or a fountain-pen cap and manage to end up with the unanswered letters still on the desk for another try the next night.

So you can understand that I have a real feeling for the fellows who have to put in their odd moments at this sort of thing all the time, even though they're helped by a number of secretaries. *I* might even misplace the secretaries. Of course, sometimes these congressional office staffs get mixed up too; and a constituent who writes to say, *Dear Congressman: I thought your speech yesterday was just frightful,* may get a reply, *Dear Sir: Thank you for your letter in support of my stand for General MacArthur. You'll be happy to know that it's the 457th one I've received.* Those things happen, and when the volume of mail is very large it's not always possible to *count* all the letters and *read* them too.

All this correspondence, chatting with visitors, and sending out of baby books and speeches goes on in addition to sitting on the floor of Congress and working in committee rooms. A senator once told me, with a cold laugh, of how he had first come to his duties in Washington bringing with him a crate full of books on history and the lives of the great, which he intended to read during his six-year term to help him become a true statesman. He not only didn't find time to open a cover, but halfway through his first term he had to move the books out to make room for the new bills and pamphlets that kept pouring in on him.

It's a busy schedule for all of them, even when they're not campaigning for

May 47

Aug 48

re-election, and I respect their efforts as exhibitions of sheer physical stamina, if nothing else. But that's not what people mean when they rise to the defense of a congressman by saying he works hard. They mean his work on legislation. And the answer to that is that there's no special virtue in working hard if they're not doing the right *kind* of work. Better that some of them should stay in bed. You and I work hard too, and so do those people who engrave

Drifting Down The River

May 49

the Lord's Prayer on the heads of pins—a mysterious occupation that I've never quite understood, but which at least does nobody any harm.

Unfortunately, some of the congressmen *do* harm, and some of the worse ones probably work harder than many of the better legislators. You have to get up pretty early in the morning to fool 150,000,000 people, and stay late at committee meetings too, if you want to make sure that a good bill is stopped or a bad one is slipped through. And if you're serving some special interests, it probably can be quite a task to get them what they want and still make it look all right to the folks back home. But to the man who's been waiting for a housing bill, let's say, and who finds it still stuck in a committee room when the congressional quitting whistle blows, it's no consolation to know that somebody—or several somebodies—had to work hard to keep it there. And when he comes home to his one-room apartment, he does not tell the little woman and the kiddies, *"My,* but those poor fellows must have had to work hard to do us out of a better deal than this!"

Well, that's the way it was with the Eightieth Congress. It may have worked hard, but the voters didn't seem to think it had applied its efforts to the right things. The "Whirlwind Finish" cartoon illustrates a few of the measures it didn't pass. And when the reports came through in the November 1948 election, many members of that Congress found that they hadn't passed either.

A lot of my stuff is about what goes on in Congress, and particularly in its committees, where legislation advances in parchesi-board fashion until it

"Remember, Papa?—The Apple"

Jan 47

Whirlwind Finish

May 48

either reaches the finish line or goes back to the beginning and has to start all over when the next Congress comes in. A two-year session seems like enough time to pass most major pieces of legislation, but there is always the last-minute rush, when several important items are swept under the carpet or piled into a closet while Congress is packing to catch the train home.

So, most of the cartoons are, as I started out to say, of a needling nature. This is a matter of as much regret to me as it may be to some good legislators who never get the recognition in pictures or in words that is given to the hatchet brigade. I suppose it works out that way for the same reason that the front pages of the newspapers feature stories about people who throw other people out of windows, but seldom run articles saying that Henry Jones, of Umpty-Ump Umptieth Street, went about his business yesterday, did a good day's work, and did *not* push anybody out of a window. And for the same reason that the congressmen themselves sometimes question people about tax cases that smell fishy, but don't call in all the good, law-abiding citizens to thank them for paying their taxes and being fine, upstanding Americans.

Cartoons don't make up into lace valentines very well, and they're not supposed to. That's not their function. I could do pictures every day of the week showing Uncle Sam resting his hand on somebody's shoulder and saying, "Well done, Insertname," and I think we'd all get pretty sick of them. They wouldn't have anything much to *say*. They'd show that many jobs were being well done, all right, but mine certainly wouldn't be one of them. So, with a lot of things going on around here and one chance to sound off every day, the cartoon is generally devoted to something that seems to me to rate some attention.

For all the senators and representatives who perform their duties ably and conscientiously in the public interest, for all the good legislation that's passed at the right time, for all the words and actions that measure up to the standards of what our national legislature should be—Congress, I love you. Here—

The reader can make a check mark in the margin at this point if he wants to, so that he can refer back to this sentiment from time to time. I've put the flowers in a pitcher of water because they're going to have to last for the course.

There's one more thing I'd like to bring up while we're on the subject. During that old horrible-example Eightieth Congress, a couple of congressional

Arsenic And Old Lace

Jan 47

"You Folks Hear Any Talk About A Housing Shortage?"

Aug 47

"I Can't Bear To Look"

Jul 51

leaders did some viewing with alarm about comments such as mine, and voiced the fear that such criticism would "destroy faith in representative government." After that particular Congress departed and one of a different political complexion came in, there were a couple of expressions of similar fears from the

"Disgusting, Ain't It?"

Jun 52

"You Wanted Controls, Didn't You?"

Aug 51

other side of the aisle. It's probably only coincidence that a few people in one party or another suddenly feel that democratic government is in danger when the criticism happens to affect them or their party. Perhaps they are concerned about this all the time but have effected a simple bi-partisan division of labor by which they take turns worrying about it. In any case they seem to leave the other branches of government to worry about criticisms of *their*

"Want To Investigate Something Real Spooky?"

Jan 51

departments, and do not feel that it is in their province to worry that criticism of the President, the Chiefs of Staff, or any other agencies might destroy the republic.

To all this kind of talk I would like to say, in a word: Nonsense! Obviously, criticisms of individuals or of acts of Congress are not a condemnation of Congress as an institution. The Congress and the rest of the government have been surviving my sketches for more than twenty years, and they have managed to stand up under a lot more and tougher criticism for something over 160 years. If faith in representative government is ever destroyed in this country, it will be because of the irresponsibility of representatives themselves—their failure to serve the best interests of the people. And if the press were to contribute to such an unhappy end, it would be by failing to speak up about those derelictions and thus displaying a matching irresponsibility.

I just wanted to get that in here.

"We'll Now Read The Minutes And The Train Schedules"

Feb 52

"There — Everything Fits"

Oct 49

3

The Face Is Familiar

THERE'S A STORY about John L. Lewis which Saul Alinsky in his unauthorized biography of the labor leader says Lewis tells on himself. Briefly it goes like this:

During a mine-contract negotiation period, when the papers were filled with articles about him, Lewis entered the elevator of the New York hotel where he was staying. Just before the elevator started up a man and a woman entered, turning immediately to "face the front." The woman had not noticed Lewis as she stepped in, and suddenly remembering that this was the hotel "where that horrible John L. Lewis is stopping" began giving her opinions of him. At her companion's nudges she only became more incensed and more voluble about Lewis, concluding her bitter remarks by saying that everybody else might be afraid of Lewis but if she ever saw him she'd tell him a thing or two.

The author quotes Lewis continuing the story with: "I brushed my eye-brows upward a little more and stepped forward in front of her saying,

A Cloud No Bigger Than A Man's Head

Aug 52

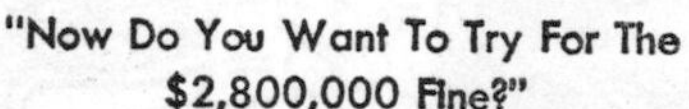
"Now Do You Want To Try For The $2,800,000 Fine?"

Apr 48

'Yes, madam, what is it you wished to tell me?' She screamed and fainted." She was carried out at the next floor, where her escort tried to revive her. And when Lewis asked if there was anything he could do to help, the escort shouted, "Yes, for God's sake go away, and I'll tell her she had a nightmare!"

Of course, all faces can't produce an effect like that, and even Lewis' wouldn't except under just the right circumstances. He generally manages to

"Let There Be Coal—Voluntarily, Of Course"

Apr 48

inject that face into the news at least once a year, and to me drawing it is a delight and a despair. People frequently comment that faces like Lewis' must be easy to do, and for a quick, recognizable cartoon likeness they are. But there is such a thing as a face being almost too easy—or having too many prominent characteristics.

Lewis' distinctive visage defies the cartoonist to improve on a caricature already well done. All the features scream for attention. If you make the eyebrows or the hair any more prominent than they are, you're going to have to take it out on the rest of the face. After all, the man has a forehead, even if we don't always approve of what goes on behind it, and this still leaves the great jowlish lower part of that countenance, which is in its way as prominent as the upper story. You'd like to exaggerate every feature, but this would only result in an oversized head too big for the bulky shoulders, which are also characteristic—even when you allow yourself a little cartoonist's license in condensing the rest of the frame. So you find yourself concentrating on items like the tilt of the hat, the thrust of the underlip, the comparatively small, slanting mouth, which cartoons almost to a rosebud in those massive features. You might almost say there's too much of John L. Lewis—which is evidently what the lady in the elevator had in mind.

The cartoon of Lewis with raised arms was done at the end of one of the psychic strikes, when the miners had left the pits without any visible or audible

"There—Now I Look Dandy"

Jul 49

Feb 50

signal from John L. himself. The "quiz show" cartoon appeared when the late Judge Goldsborough fined the U.M.W. twice the amount he had fined that organization for a previous strike.

Senator McCarran's face is not as well known as Lewis', but it figures in many of these cartoons. In going through some photographs of him on one occasion, I found some that showed him in need of a once-over-lightly, felt that the stubble fitted the character of him I was presenting in the drawing, and have been picturing him that way ever since. I understand that the senator resents that light beard more than anything in the cartoons themselves, and prides himself on being something of a dude. To me he is the kind of dude that used to be portrayed in the old two-color covers of the nickel magazines —the covers that sometimes featured a tramp character looking genteel as he held in hand, with pinky extended, a toothpick on which a cigar butt was impaled.

In the cartoon, "There—Now I Look Dandy," I gave McCarran a shave—or had him give himself one, but I doubt whether this pleased him any better. His dislike for these cartoons was evidenced in a somewhat surprising way when he gave as one reason for trying to lop $10,000,000 off a State Department appropriation the fact that the department had distributed abroad a number of my cartoons kicking Communism around. Of course these cartoons had nothing to do with domestic policies or with Senator McCarran shaved or unshaved. Apparently he was mad about *any* of my stuff being sent overseas, even in the fight against Communism. A full vote of the Senate rode him down and restored the appropriation he had cut.

On the subject of beards, Senator McCarthy seems to be one of those people who have a natural five-o'clock shadow, and from a cartoon standpoint on him it looks appropriate.

I must say that the few public figures who feel that I've mussed them up in my drawings would unquestionably "take a better picture" on my drawing board if I thought they represented great statesmanship. Caricatures are not studio portraits, and aren't meant to be. They are exaggerations and sometimes personal interpretations just as much as the cartoon itself. They scarcely flatter a subject at any time, and the cartoonist sometimes does a kind of Picture of Dorian Gray which presents a character that the subject himself does not see when he looks in the mirror.

Actually I don't think that physical appearance is much of an indication of character, and I once pasted up a batch of unfamiliar photos of assorted professional people, con men, legislators, and racketeers to see if anyone could tell which was which—and of course no one could. I think we generally "recognize telltale signs" in physical appearance after we've developed a dislike

"You See, Friend? I Told You Your Watch Was No Good"

Oct 46

"Is That Me Talking?"

Nov 47

for other reasons. I have a friend who, during Roosevelt's last two terms in office, used to tell me that F. D. R.'s eyes were "set close together" and that this was "a bad sign."

Senator Taft is a frequent subject for cartoons because he makes himself so. Whether you like him or not, he's a prominent figure and generally in the

"Ike!"

Aug 51

"Into The Wild Blue Yonder"

Jun 52

"And Who's Giving Who Away, Now?"

Dec 46

"A Sensational Announcement, Folks!—"

Oct 51

news, even if only to issue a statement contradicting something he said a short time before. I don't know him, but like many of the people I've met whose policies I've had occasion to criticize in the cartoons he may be pleasant enough personally. But in the cartoons I'm interested only in people as they represent issues. My general feeling about Taft as a political figure is that he's like some remarkable calculating machine that can pull statistics out of its innards at any moment, can add, subtract, multiply, and divide them while other minds are reaching for pencil and paper, and can be depended upon almost invariably to come up with the wrong answer.

The cartoons about him have been more popular than most, and requests for the drawings come from members of both parties. Some assorted Tafts from 1946 to the present are included here.

If the senator sometimes slips up on the Taft record, it's only fair to mention that once I did the same thing. The cartoon of Taft and Bricker as alternate bridegrooms was drawn in 1946, and referred to his having stepped aside to let Bricker run for the Presidential nomination in 1944, after Taft had made his initial try in 1940. But in 1951, when I was showing Mr. Taft carefully placing his hat in the ring, I forgot about the Robert Alfonso and Gaston routine of nearly eight years before, and drew hats representing *four* bids for the Presidency. When this cartoon was reprinted in the St. Louis *Post-Dispatch,* on Fitzpatrick's day off, it ran alongside a two-column editorial headed "Taft's Third Try." They heard about that extra hat—and so did I.

In the cartoon of Attlee and the pipe, drawn when he was re-elected by a

Feb 50

Dec 51

narrow margin, the cigar seemed enough to suggest Churchill. But since the whole thing depended on recognition of Attlee, I played it safe and labeled him, to avoid any possible confusion with the bald, moustached face of Public, which is more familiar to cartoon readers. The other Attlee cartoon hardly comes under the heading of "familiar faces," but it appeared a day or so later.

Feb 50

Feb 50

The adjoining version of the same drawing shows how a Canadian newspaper which carries my stuff contrived to cover the Prime Minister's embarrassment.

There is a little suggestion of Will Rogers in President Truman's face, particularly the nose and lower lip, and he has some of the same folksy approach in impromptu talks. After F.D.R. there was some feeling that Truman was not "a good subject for caricature"; but the fact is that while some faces lend

themselves to cartooning more than others, all caricatures look better as they and the subject become more familiar.

General Eisenhower, whose pictures sometimes make him look quite old and sometimes almost boyish, didn't seem to caricature very well at first, but he probably will. Each cartoonist develops a formula for a face that comes up frequently, and the reader finally becomes so well acquainted with the pattern that the subject and the caricature seem to look more and more like each other all the time.

Governor Stevenson's features make him a good subject for a comparatively easy likeness, and as those features are drawn more often they will become increasingly exaggerated.

When minor exaggerations of "characteristics" become accepted, the cartoonists often proceed to stretch them a little further. In the early cartoons of F.D.R., the chin became increasingly prominent. The Calvin Coolidge nose was not so *very* long and pointed, but when the cartoonists seized on it as a distinguishing feature it grew to look something like Pinocchio's. President Hoover's features, on the other hand, became more compressed in the caricatures, until his face was sometimes represented by a few tight lines in the middle of a circle.

The ultimate in symbolism or simplification was probably reached by Daumier, who drew pear-shaped caricatures of King Louis Philippe, and eventually represented the sovereign simply *as* a pear, with no other identification.

The late Senator Wherry used to be known as the "merry mortician" because of a business interest he'd had. This is probably what was in the back of my mind when I pictured him in the cartoon undertaker's outfit shown in one of these drawings. I continued using that costume, not to make fun of his former business interest, but because his role in the Senate was generally that of a man ready to bury most of the measures that were introduced. He was a strongly partisan man, but one not without humor.

The cartoonist—or at least this one—is a little disconcerted when he does a cartoon that's intended to take the hide off some political figure, and then hears the subject of that cartoon on the telephone, chuckling, laughing, and asking for the drawing. This happens, and there have been times when I hastily thumbed through the newspaper with one hand, while holding the phone with the other, to make sure we were both talking about the same cartoon. Sometimes partisans of one political leader or another will berate me for a drawing that the politician himself thinks is wonderful. This may be good public relations—sportsmanship and all that—or, more likely, a simple pleasure at being pictured in the papers in some more-or-less funny drawing. In any case, I never hear from the subjects themselves when they are unhappy about the cartoons. I might learn that they've blown their tops in committee meetings, said something in Congress or outside, or complained to the editor. But the only time I hear from them directly is when they like a cartoon, or at least want the drawing.

Occasionally the reporters hear from the subjects of cartoons, as in the case of a 1952 drawing, reproduced in a later chapter, that showed the McCarran Committee as a group of medieval, black-robed, hooded inquisitors in a torture chamber. On the day that one appeared, the Washington *Post* reporter covering the committee walked into its hearing room and was greeted coldly by a senator who growled, without any preliminary conversation, "Which one is me?" At the reporter's place along the press table another committee member had carefully laid a poker obtained from a near-by fireplace.

One former senator has hanging in his law office, along with pictures of his family, a single cartoon, drawn by an artist in his home state, which lampooned him when he first ran for the Senate. He still enjoys it, possibly because he had the last laugh on the cartoonist.

There are times when the caricatures are double-featured, like the one shown here of Taft and the boy on the train. I used doubles again in a cartoon showing another senator sitting across a desk from himself—one figure representing him in his capacity as senator, the other representing him in his capacity as the recipient of money for outside work.

Just to balance things, there have also been some in which the subject of the cartoon wasn't there at all. When Senator McFarland became Senate

"Tsk Tsk! Another Suicide" — *Mar 49*

"Never Saw Him Before In My Life" — *Sep 47*

"Don't Be Ridiculous. Nobody Is A Dinosaur Any More"

Jun 52

majority leader in 1951, I did a drawing of a non-existent leadership married to a non-existent working majority, pictured as empty bride and groom costumes being showered with rice.

A few years earlier there was occasion to include in a cartoon a man named Ernie Adamson, then counsel for the Committee on Un-American Activities. I had never seen him; and when I couldn't even find a photo of him this strengthened a theory—formed after reading some of the statements attributed

"Pardon Me, Mister—Do You Know What Time It Is?"

Aug 46

Reading The Minutes

Jun 47

to him—that there couldn't be any such person. So in the cartoon his head appeared as a balloon on a string which stuck up out of an empty collar. The face was neither familiar nor important, and the substitute served to convey an opinion about him.

"Want To See Me Blow Out Everything With One Puff?"

Aug 49

Tick-Tock Tick-Tock

Jan 49

"Don't Mind Me—Just Go Right On Talking"

Feb 47

Among less personal characterizations, the one of Mr. Atom—based on the bomb of the same name—is a figure that just grew. He wasn't planned as a continuing character, but after his first appearance he kept muscling into the pictures as a warning that he wasn't going to be permanently on our side alone and that if he weren't controlled he could cut loose on the whole world.

There's a sort of law of diminishing returns on the frequent use of a "heavy" character like this. If you don't watch this type of fellow, he'll get to hamming it up, burlesquing himself, and becoming a funny, likable guy. Also, as Alexander Pope wrote about another monster:

> . . . seen too oft, familiar with her face,
> We first endure, then pity, then embrace.

I felt a good deal of satisfaction when people used to tell me, with flattering exaggeration, that the Atom character gave them the shivers. But when I began hearing about "that cute Mr. Atom you draw," I gave him longer rest periods. And while the Communists were plugging their "peace petition" which condemned only atomic weapons, I kept him completely corked up so that he wouldn't get himself mixed up with a carefully twisted viewpoint. He continues to throw his weight around in the cartoons once in a while and raises his head here and there in this volume to remind us that he's still present and big as life—or death.

Cartoons, and comedy in general, have come a long way from the misleading cliché characters used in the days when Frenchmen were portrayed with parted black beards, Englishmen with monocles, and when any foreign accent or presumed "racial characteristic" was considered hilarious. By now it's pretty well recognized that people of various races and nationalities are not characters out of early musical shows, and that the nations of the world aren't eagles, lions, roosters, or other residents of zoos or barnyards.

"I'll Be Glad To Lend You My Sickle" Number One Boy

Aug 51 *Dec 50*

One old national figure that survives in these drawings is Uncle Sam. A figure to represent the U.S. wouldn't look much like that today, when you can walk around any corner without bumping into someone with chin whiskers or a beaver hat. But he's been streamlined enough to lose the stripes from his pants and the stars from his vest; and the hat has been smoothed and polished into a later-model topper. The reason I keep using the Uncle Sam character is that he's instantly recognizable and is accepted for the convenient cartoon

"There Ain't No Such Animal"

Apr 52

symbol he is, without giving any really misleading impression about representing national characteristics.

There's no question about representations of totalitarian governments which in each case can be pictured by the face of "The Leader." Hitler *was* the Nazi government, and Stalin *is* the government of Soviet Russia. He undoubtedly looks fatherly and noble in the drawings over there, where they can't caricature

"Oh, No—Not Again—I'm Tired"

HERBLOCK

Mar 51

**" 'Tis But Thy Name That Is My Enemy; . . .
O! Be Some Other Name: What's In A Name?"**

Feb 50

HERBLOCK

him anyhow. But more of the cunning and ruthlessness comes out in that face as we see it. Of course, if governments were to be represented by the old animal-kingdom figures, I'd be strongly tempted to take up a suggestion advanced by Eugene Meyer—that the proper beast for Soviet Russia today is the bear in sheep's clothing.

The faces for Mr. Public and Wrong-Guy Congressmen are variations of old

"Okay, Kid—Now All You've Got To Do Is Make Good"

Feb 47

"Good Morning, Sir. You, As The Head Of The House—"

Jan 51

familiar cartoon characters. The Congressional figure represents congressmen in what I consider to be their less enlightened moments. Sometimes this figure represents the majority, sometimes a group or committee within Congress. He's a general, all-purpose caricature of a legislator with a foot in the bucket. When

The Driver's Seat

Nov 50

"Ah, There's Nothing Like An Open Fire"

Dec 51

I do a generalized figure of a congressman as a statesman, of course the hair is trimmed, the chin firms up, and he looks quite noble.

Under a parliamentary system, cartoons are more easily personalized. A Prime Minister and his cabinet *are* the majority party and the parliament, and when they stop being that they go out. But the President of the United States obviously can't be used to represent the entire government including Congress. And the political-party symbols or the majority and minority leaders in Congress can't always be used to represent that branch—or even the parties in it. We operate under an every-man-for-himself system, where opinions and policies can't always be pinned down to a few individuals; and an all-purpose Wrong-Guy figure is extremely handy for representing what I consider to be the backward boys of both parties on any issue.

It's been proposed from time to time that the party lines be straightened out and that the relationship between Republicans and anti-Administration Democrats be legitimatized with a sort of marriage ceremony at the polls. If this ever takes place, the union might produce a new cartoon character. Perhaps there should be one anyhow to represent the coalition in Congress. Meanwhile, we have cartoons like the Romeo and Juliet one on this subject.

The elephant and the donkey are two more familiar features that have come down through the years and still are very active. When Thomas Nast first drew them, they pictured the relative size of the parties' votes in an election, and I think also conveyed his feeling at the time about the dignity and nobility of one of the parties as compared with the other. But they've long ago lost their original significance. Like Uncle Sam they may seem rather incongruous now, but they also have the virtue of being clearly recognizable—and, what's more, these personalized animals are a lot of fun. They have acquired a certain legitimacy because the political parties themselves make use of them. When nature holds the mirror up to art that way, I suppose the cartoonists might as well accept the situation.

4

A Walk Around Constitution Hall

ONE OF THE THINGS that make life complicated—one of the things, as a matter of fact, practically *dedicated* to making life complicated—is the practice of Mumbo-Jumbo. Since the word is used here in a broader sense than the dictionary defines it, perhaps I'd better explain what I mean by it. Mumbo-Jumbo, as I use the term, is the transference of devotion from a set of principles to the symbols and rituals that are built up around them. It's the business of taking over a good, sound idea, building an elaborate shell around it, then carefully removing the already wilting idea and beating its brains out with the shell.

For example—suppose several primitive tribes decide to get together and live in harmony. They hit upon the idea of gathering rocks from their respective areas to build a monument symbolizing their mutual brotherhood and common belief in some kind of deity. They all work together building this pile of rocks and then meet once in a while to bow their heads before it. Well, this is where Mumbo-Jumbo moves in.

Pretty soon some of the men get the idea that if you bow low enough to rap your head on the rocks this shows that you are a little more devout and brotherly than the rest of the boys. The rocks themselves are now coming to be the important thing—the size and number of lumps on the head becoming marks of distinction and high standing in the community. From here it's but a short step to the insistence that everybody should have lumps on his head whether he likes it or not, and anybody with a normal noggin is an evil fellow. Soon it is considered a brotherly and patriotic act to bounce rocks off your neighbor's skull to make a better man of him. And, finally, the complete destruction of a neighbor in that manner will be considered the highest form of brotherly expression, and will guarantee the pitcher of the fatal rock a special heaven with sixteen wives, betel nuts every day, and all the rocks he can throw.

That's Mumbo-Jumbo.

Anybody who's ever had a garden knows that the planting of the seeds is only a minor part of the work and that the rest consists of cultivation and the beating off of bugs, fungi, and weeds which would choke off the plant growth. I think the story of human progress is something like this—a part of it consisting of the launching of new and better ideas, and the rest of it being the eternal chore of fighting rot, scraping off barnacles, and keeping those good ideas in operating condition.

Mumbo-Jumbo creeps up in practically every field of endeavor. It gets into the arts when the flourishes and curlicues of technique become more important than the message, the picture, or the work as a whole; into medicine when the operation becomes more important than the patient; into religion when the form alone is substituted for the spirit; and into governments and organizations when symbols, protocol, slogans, and prestige devices crowd out the ideas of general welfare.

The Constitution and the Declaration of Independence have now been put into new, scientifically devised, temperature-controlled, decay-resistant cases; and we're all glad to know that they're being preserved. But there are no gadgets that can insure the preservation of the spirit of those documents. That's a job that comes harder and that never ends. A part of the price of liberty is eternal vigilance against Mumbo-Jumbo as well as against other forms of tyranny. And there are always among us some to whom the Flag as a physical Thing is so much more important than the freedom it stands

"Go Back! Wrong Boat!"

May 47

"Yoo Hoo! Boys! Are You Displaying The Flag Properly?"

Apr 52

for that they are ready to beat up or clap into jail anyone who is not sufficiently quick on the draw in saluting it.

I've done several cartoons about the Daughters of the American Revolution, generally at the time of their annual conventions in Washington. And some readers have told me that they look forward to the D.A.R. cartoon each year, just after the cherry blossoms. This is flattering, but I never meant

"Sh! After A While They'll Go Away"

Jul 47

those cartoons to be a perennial job, and I don't sharpen my pencil and rub my hands together in happy anticipation of those conventions. As far as I'm concerned, the D.A.R. conclave is just like any other meeting in town, when delegates blossom out in badges and ribbons, fill the hotels, and occupy a lot of the taxicabs. They can go ahead with their work, I'll go ahead with mine,

The Shot Heard Round The Immediate Vicinity

Apr 49

HERBLOCK

and I'll just have lunch at the office while the restaurants are overflowing with them.

But before the ladies adjourn they always pass a flurry of resolutions. These are reported at some length in the papers, and that's how those cartoons come to be drawn.

Just according to the law of averages the D.A.R. should some year put through a whole list of resolutions that would all strike me as being bell-ringers and make me want to walk through the Mayflower lobby clapping them on the back till their corsages fall off. But it never happens; and I think I've figured out why. It's that Mumbo-Jumbo business. When an organization starts out by assuming that there's some inherent virtue in having ancestors who were here early, it's getting itself buttoned up wrong right at the start.

The Daughters evidently think highly of their ancestors—at least *as* ancestors, although they and the ancestors probably couldn't stand each other if they were contemporaries. Because those forebears founded a nation on the idea that ancestry didn't make any difference. That was the new idea and that's what made the whole thing great. Oddly enough, some of the descendants are revolutionists of a sort themselves—in dignified, completely unaware revolt against the ideas of the forefathers they revere. I liked the little newspaper item about Senator Henry Cabot Lodge, Jr., who, when asked by a reporter if he was a direct descendant of the original American Lodges, guessed that he was but said he'd rather not talk about it because "that sort of thing seems so un-American."

"Drop In Any Time"

May 52

"And Why Did The Administration Let So Many Foreigners Get Into The United Nations?"

HERBLOCK

Sep 48

Well, if you believe it's important to have American ancestors all the way back, you can't get much whipped up about the idea of taking in recent arrivals, even though these immigrants may be fired by the ideals that led the founding fathers to establish this country—and closer to them in spirit than a lot of the natives. If you're concerned only with the physical ground the ancestors walked, you're not likely to get excited about having a world government some day, even though the parallel between this and the union of former American colonies is so striking it hits you between the lenses of your lorgnette. When you really become absorbed with the Flag as a Thing and the country as an Exclusive Organization, you're not likely to take a bright view of the United Nations or the display of its banner. One year a D.A.R. delegate delivered a stirring speech demanding that the government "put teeth in the flag code" for proper display of the Stars and Stripes. And I suppose it was natural that a group so concerned about this should be a little snappish about the hoisting of the U.N. insignia.

I haven't wanted to belabor the D.A.R here any more than I've wanted to in the cartoons. But it often exemplifies that Mumbo-Jumbo stuff I've been talking about, and because it happens to hold its annual conventions in Washington I've given it more attention than a number of other organizations which have some of the same virtues and defects. All of them are made up mostly of pleasant, sincere people, earnestly patriotic according to their views; and if their delegates are sometimes misguided in their zeal, the membership also perform many good works which don't always bring forth editorial comment.

When Dorothy Maynor sang in Constitution Hall in February 1952, this performance marked the end of a discriminatory policy which had kept Marian Anderson from appearing on this D.A.R. stage in 1939. And the D.A.R. never had a policy of segregation or discrimination—even during the years when owners of some other public halls in Washington did—regarding *audiences* in its auditorium. For things like this I think the Daughters rate a salute.

Several patriotic organizations have been generally "anti-immigration." The refugee problem is still a most important one, but at the time the cartoons in this section were drawn the immediate issue was that of admitting displaced persons. One of the cartoons on this subject which brought some unusual reactions was that of the ghostly soldier and the D.P. child. There were a few letters which described this drawing as an "insult to the Gold Star mothers" —none of these letters coming from people who could classify as members of that group. But the people I heard from who had actually lost members of their families in the war all said that they liked the cartoon.

One letter that gave me considerable thought came from a lady in Chicago

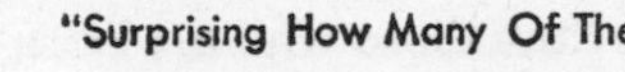

"They Didn't Ask Me Who Should Get The Trip, Kid"

Oct 47

"Surprising How Many Of Them Don't Come In"

Feb 49

who wrote that her son had been killed in the war, that she had seen the cartoon in the Chicago *Sun-Times,* and that she would like me to tell her how to go about adopting a D.P. child. Distressed by the idea that she had probably misunderstood the drawing and might be acting out of some mistaken sense of duty, I phoned her and explained that the cartoon simply advocated Congressional action to aid the living, and that the farthest thing from my mind was that people like herself should take on additional burdens. But she hadn't been under any misapprehension at all, and told me that the cartoon had given her the idea of adopting some European child to share the home to which her son would never return.

There are a lot of people in the groups who oppose immigration who would, I suppose, be somewhat shocked at the suggestion that many of the newer arrivals to this country are better Americans than some of the old-line inhabitants. But it's true.

It's not necessary to call the roll of outstanding first- and second-generation Americans who helped to make the country so great, or to list the names on the headstones of those who died in our wars, or to cite the learned scientists of various countries who contributed, among other things, to our atomic research. The principle of immigration is good enough without these.

The immigrants aren't all potential heroes or brainy scientists, and they don't need to be. A lot of them may not be well educated by schoolroom standards. But people who have seen tyranny close up sometimes understand freedom better than those who are born to it. And they can speak the language of Washington, Adams, and Jefferson without even knowing the words.

"All of us," said Franklin D. Roosevelt in a speech on the subject, "are descended from immigrants." I think it's well to remember this, not only for the sake of possible future citizens but for our own welfare. For, expansive and full of Christian charity as we may feel about letting in "outsiders," the fact

"What Happened To The One We Used To Have?"

Oct 46

is that we need them as much as they need us. It is this new blood and continual regeneration of the original American spirit that has contributed to our strength and kept us from developing national hardening of the arteries. And it is this fusion of races and nationalities and descendants of immigrants old and new that has made us the hope of the world and offered a working pattern for the world of the future. If we want to keep thinking of ourselves as the hope of the world and want others to look at us in that light, I think we'd better remember how we got that way in the first place.

"How'm I Doin'?"

July 4, 47

5

Side Show

THE VISITOR who comes to Washington expecting to find a lot of musical revues and stay-up-late spots is pretty sure to be disappointed; and he may spend the rest of his stay sulking in his hotel room, snapping at the chambermaids and getting quietly potted. There's no need for anybody to break himself up that way. We have a lot of great shows here. But in this Hollywood of government and politics they're a special kind, and are quietly billed in the papers in a couple of classified ad-type paragraphs like this:

In Congress

TODAY

Senate

Meets at 10 a. m.

Committees: **Judiciary Subcommittee,** 1:30 p. m., open. S.J. Res. 130—To amend Constitution regarding making of treaties. **D. C. Subcommittee,** 2:30 p. m., open. S. 2734—Additional judge for D. C. Juvenile Court: S. 3258—To amend D. C. Code: H.R. 5768—To regulate boxing contests in D. C. Room P-38, Capitol. **Judiciary,** 10:30 a. m., exec. General committee business. Room 424, Senate Office Bldg. **Post Office and Civil Service Subcommittee,** 10 a. m., exec. Postal matters. Room 135, Senate Office Bldg. **Appropriations Subcommittee,** 10 a. m., exec. Armed Service bill. Room 224, Senate Office Bldg. **Appropriations Subcommittee,** 10:30 a. m., exec. Civil functions bill. Room F-37 Capitol.

House

Meets at noon.

Committees: **Appropriations,** 10 a. m., exec. Subcommittee on Mutual Security and Military Construction. Committee Room, Capitol: **Armed Services,** 10 a. m., open. S. 3019—To extend to reserve and retired officers now on active duty the application of the special inducement pay provided thereby to doctors and dentists. Room 313-A Old. Bldg.; **Education and Labor,** 10:30 a. m., exec. Bailey Subcommittee on school construction bill. Room 429 Old Bldg.; **Interior and Insular Affairs,** 10 a. m., open. Engle subcommittee on H.R. 6804 providing that the costs of certain functions served by reclamation projects shall be nonreimbursable under the Federal Reclamation laws. Room 1324 New Bldg.: **Judiciary,** 10 a. m., open. Walter Subcommittee on private immigration bills. Room 327 Old Bldg.: **Judiciary,** 10 a. m., open. Lane subcommittee on private claim bills. Room 346 Old Bldg.: **Merchant Marine and Fisheries,** 10 a. m., open. Shelley Subcommittee to review redetermination of vessels sales prices of SS Constitution and Independence. Room 219 Old Bldg.: **Teague Committee Investigating Education and Loan Guaranty Programs under the G.I. bill,** 10 a. m., open. To hear Maurice Weiss, vice president, Spiller Construction Co., in connection with the operation of the veterans' home loan guaranty program in the Washington metropolitan area. Room 445 Old Bldg.; **Interstate and Foreign Commerce, 10 a. m.,** Open. H. Con. Res. 19—To express the sense of the Congress that a civilian physical fitness and training program should be established to the interest of national security. Congressman Hedrick of West Virginia, author of the resolution; John Core of Huntington, W. Va., and possibly the Mayor of Miami, will be heard. Room 1334 New Bldg.

In the deadpan listing above there's none of that stuff about how these performances will chill you, thrill you, knock you out of your seat, and send you home blubbering to yourself. You wouldn't know that some of these are the committee meetings that are getting all the big notices in the front pages of the paper at all. They include the big shows, though, complete with comedy, tragedy, and suspense—and what casts! Everybody from the country's most distinguished citizens to crooks, Commies, and dope addicts. We've had movie stars in them too. In person.

The investigating committees sometimes go on the road, sometimes their hearings are broadcast, and of course when the Kefauver Committee brought the Congressional version of *Guys and Dolls* to television the whole country found out why people around here often stand in line to get a glimpse of these matinees.

The cartoons in this section recall a few memorable moments of Congressional drama from the days before a million nervous hands fiddled with dials to bring into focus the even more nervous hands of Mr. Frank Costello.

Leaving aside for the moment the permanent, long-run Committee on Un-American Activities, which is sort of the *Tobacco Road* of public hearings, the smash hit of the 1947 season was the Brewster-Hughes investigation, represented here by the cartoon "I Shot an Arrow—." Modestly billed as an investigation into wartime plane contracts, this one was generally recognized as an Epic Struggle between Senator Owen Brewster, friend of Pan-American's Juan Trippe, and—in this corner—Howard Hughes, head of Trans World Airlines, movie producer, and discoverer of Jane Russell.

There was a sequel to this clash in the 1950 investigation of wire-tapping, when it was alleged that there had been eavesdropping on Mr. Hughes' telephone conversations in Washington. Whatever may have been accomplished by such an illegal business, if it took place, Mr. Hughes did not seem to be at any noticeable disadvantage at the time, when he delivered a socko performance and ran off with the show.

Mr. Hughes, who was in California when the fireworks started, took to the

I Shot An Arrow Into The Air,
It Fell To Earth, I Knew Not Where

Aug 47

"Now, That's Real Art—Almost Like A Photograph"

Jun 47

air by radio as well as by plane, carrying the fight to his opponent. After several hot August days of testimony, during which the senator from Maine heard himself accused of attempted blackmail, Brewster recessed the hearings indefinitely and took off for the tall cool woods of his native state.

Less gaudy as a show but definitely in the Oscar class for a singularly restrained and moving performance was the inquisition of David Lilienthal earlier the same year, when he was up for confirmation as chairman of the

"It's Sure Hard To Get Help These Days"

Oct 47

Atomic Energy Commission. The heavy in this drama was Senator McKellar, who nursed an old grudge from Lilienthal's T.V.A. days, and harassed the nominee unmercifully. When Mr. Lilienthal replied with his moving statement on democracy which began, "This I do carry in my head, Senator . . . ," he stopped the show, even temporarily stopped Senator McKellar, and set off a kind of chain reaction of popular enthusiasm.

Something that congressmen might consider when they are in a mood for self-examination is the fact that in hearings like the two mentioned above the public sympathy has been with the "defendants" who struck back, rather than on the side of the legislators supposed to be representing the public interest. Abuses of authority by individual members eventually kick back on a committee, on the Senate, and on Congress as a whole.

The Lilienthal hearings occasioned a couple of the several cartoons I've done on the subject of getting able men for public offices. In part this is made difficult by a few legislators who act as if they feel there must be something wrong with anybody who's willing to serve his country in any capacity except as a member of Congress.

I don't know how much fat could be trimmed from the federal payroll but I've seen a lot of able, conscientious people around here, some working for the government at a sacrifice to themselves. Oddly enough, when some of them get fed up with abuse and comparatively low salaries they are frequently offered much more lucrative positions by some of the same private executives who condemn public servants as "shiftless bureaucrats living offa the public."

The cartoon "Now That's Real Art—" harks back to a tawdry burlesque performance in Congress; and as a guy who once took some drawing lessons, I want to get in a note on the subject. President Truman had referred to so-called modern art as "ham-and-egg art." A little later, when this cartoon was drawn, a Congressional committee was going somewhat farther than that in ridiculing the paintings in an exhibition of American art which the State Department had sent abroad. I don't think it's possible to generalize about "modern" or "old-fashioned" art—both categories being so vague and including so great an assortment of work by so many artists of varying abilities. Whatever the merits of these particular exhibition paintings, the congressmen who indulged in cultural demagoguery, vying with one another in making sport of them, certainly weren't qualified to judge them. Well, the footnote on that performance is this:

The exhibition had been well received abroad. When it was broken up—as a result of Congressional criticism—the pictures were purchased by several distinguished museums and educational institutions. And if the government had been out to make a profit on the paintings, it could have sold them to private collectors at much higher prices than it had paid for them.

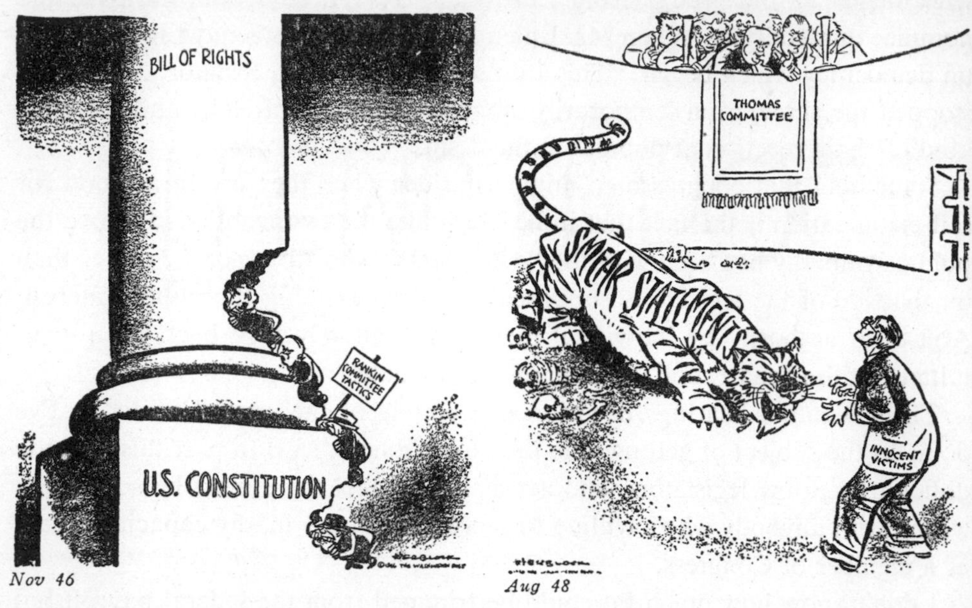

Nov 46

Aug 48

The balance of these cartoons is on the continuous performance of the Committee on Un-American Activities, which reached its height—or depth—during 1947 and '48. Looking over them now, I'm surprised that the Alice-in-Wonderland theme didn't figure in any of them. This was probably because the subject didn't seem to fall into the Innocent Fun Department. But certainly this committee's operations resembled a mad party. And if nobody was pushed into a teapot, at least the chairman ended up in the jug—and that, as Alice might have said, was curious enough.

Watching some of the klieg-lighted hearings conducted by J. Parnell Thomas, I might not have been too surprised to hear the words *Off with their heads!* or *Sentence first and verdict afterward!* The manner in which the hearings were held at least suggested that this group felt, *"I'll be judge, I'll be jury,"* (*Said cunning old Fury*); *"I'll try the whole cause, and condemn you to death."* Not real death, of course, and not real heads rolling. But for the reputations of a number of patriotic Americans—as well as some Communists indiscriminately mixed in to create the maximum confusion—it was close enough. The tiger cartoon illustrates what seemed to me to be one of the worst features of the methods used in these investigations.

One reason for the Wonderland wanderings of this committee was the absent-minded way in which it was set up. Congress said that it was to investigate un-Americanism and left the Committee to decide what that was. This group's idea of un-Americanism turned out roughly to be whatever disagreed with the political opinions of its members. And *roughly* is the word I mean. But however much they may have wanted conformity in others they certainly seemed to believe in free expression for themselves—individual members sometimes tossing off public statements which were news even to the other members of the same committee.

Most of the time the committee seemed to regard itself as a court. It told

"It's Okay—We're Hunting Communists"

Oct 47

witnesses that they were in court, that they were on trial before "the great bar of public opinion." But if a defendant asked for the rights he'd have in any court, it quickly slipped out of its invisible black robes and into its invisible Sherlock Holmes cape. After all, it said in effect, this is not a court, my good man; it's simply an investigating committee Looking for Facts.

It was more consistent in its assertions regarding "pitiless publicity." In this it seemed to have a keen interest. And its members were not reluctant to share in the bright white light until it got a little *too* hot and pitiless.

Like the Alice-in-Wonderland characters who painted the white roses red, the members of this group didn't mind splattering the cleanest of reputations to get the color effects they wanted. And when it didn't do the paint job itself, it had "friendly witnesses" free to testify with immunity from libel, who could swing the brushes for them. The accused were, of course, seldom given the opportunity to reply—even if there was any hope that a reply might catch up with the original charge.

Among many good Americans who shared this experience was Lowell Mellett, distinguished columnist and former editor of the Washington *News*. He was surprised to find himself sideswiped in one of Mr. Thomas' statements and wrote several times requesting an opportunity to appear before the committee. The letters went unanswered, but Thomas later announced publicly that he was going to have Mr. Mellett *subpoenaed*. Since he was covering the hearings anyhow, Mr. Mellett daily came prepared to be called on, and even

"If You Ask Me, It's Un-American"

Oct 47

"Whatever You Do, Don't Fling Me Into Dat Brier Patch"

Jun 48

took to inquiring when he would be given his chance to appear as a witness. But he was never called. Nor were many others who had received the same hit-and-run treatment. Dr. Edward U. Condon, head of the U.S. Bureau of Standards, was frequently attacked by the committee and just as frequently cracked back at it in the public prints. In 1951, long after J. Parnell Thomas had been sent to prison, Dr. Condon resigned his position with honor to become research director of the Corning Glass Works. In 1952, four years after the committee had begun attacking him, it finally called Dr. Condon to testify.

The movie cartoon appeared during one of the many investigations of Hollywood—always sure-fire headline material. This much-publicized probe showed that there were some Communists in the movie industry—but it produced no evidence that movie screens had been reddened by anything more than the conventional use of Technicolor. The investigations did, however, succeed in intimidating an industry already afraid of its own shadow-pictures and generally nervous about any theme in which Boy Meets Idea.

In 1948 the committee revealed to the public indisputable evidence of the existence of espionage in the government ten years earlier. This came in the form of the "pumpkin paper" microfilms produced by Whittaker Chambers in support of his charges against Alger Hiss. I don't think that this disclosure by the committee is to be minimized; but such corroboration of testimony was the exception rather than the rule.

The ultimate conviction of Hiss was cited in attempts to justify all the mis-

"We Got To Burn The Evil Spirits Out Of Her" **The Devil Was Sick, The Devil A Monk Would Be**

May 48 *Dec 48*

deeds of this committee and of any groups that employed its methods. And some of the less scrupulous supporters of these methods even tried to imply that those who were critical of any of the committee's tactics must be "defenders of Alger Hiss." Which is something like saying that if you are against lynching you must be in favor of rape or murder.

In a somewhat more logical vein it has often been said that the conviction of Hiss was worth all the *money* that had been spent by the Committee on Un-American Activities. But this misses the point. As the old saying goes—it's not the money, it's the principle. The question is whether this committee could justify in any way the unnecessary smearing and intimidating of innocent people, the kind of confusion which it and the Communists helped to create about the nature and strength of Communism in the U.S., the use of its power for political purposes, and the headline-grabbing which interfered with real detection of Communism by trained agents. The whole of this committee's procedure was contrary to American standards of conduct, under which you don't mow down citizens at random even to get a gangster. There are undoubtedly some Communists, as well as crooks, thieves, and maybe a murderer or two, among all the people listed in a big-city phone book. But you don't indict every telephone subscriber to get them.

Chairman Thomas, whose payroll-padding proclivities were exposed in Drew Pearson's column, was convicted and sentenced in 1949. It would be unfair to charge all the committee members with the guilt by association which they so frequently used against others. They were not responsible for the financial finagling in the chairman's Congressional office. But he and they were responsible for the manner in which the committee overrode the rights of innocent individuals, and lowered the standards of Congressional investigations. And to me that's the greater crime.

By the end of 1948, when the "devil-was-sick" cartoon appeared, even a couple of the Committee members conceded the need for some kind of reform.

What's been wrong with the Committee on Un-American Activities and a few other investigative groups might best be summed up by calling attention to what they have *not* been. Noting that bills for reform of committee procedures were first introduced in 1947—the period we're dealing with here—the 1951 Senate Subcommittee on Ethical Standards in Government, headed by Senator Paul Douglas, recommended as a code of fair play:

> . . . withholding of publicity regarding accusations or charges against individuals until there is evidence to support the charges; giving advance notice to individuals, wherever possible, if they are to be attacked in public hearings; giving such individuals an opportunity to be present, to cross-examine witnesses and to make an immediate reply; and an avoidance of intimidation or browbeating of witnesses.

When it is not known what line a witness will take, it is not possible to avoid some unfairness to persons who may be attacked in the testimony. But since unwarranted inferences are so easily drawn and bad news travels fast, every effort should be made to achieve a high degree of responsibility and fairness in all committee proceedings. *Experience has shown that such standards of fairness do not interfere with effective committee investigations,* and it is particularly important that Congress, which is the popular branch of government, should take the lead in respecting the rights of individuals in insuring the validity of its findings.

The italics are mine.

The last couple of cartoons in this section—about the stooge and the former leopard—were prompted by the committee's star-witness system in its performances, which glorified the ex-Commie the way Ziegfeld used to glorify the American girl. After all the hours I've spent over a hot drawing board dealing with this group, I don't want to kiss it good-by here without a word about that particular innovation in committee shows. I mean the unquestioned acceptance of testimony by ex-Commies, even those who sometimes still seem to commit a little perjury among friends, without the support of real evidence.

I hope I'm as charitable as the next one, and I don't think former crooks and former Communists should be denied any opportunity to straighten up and fly right. Some of the "ex's" undoubtedly can give and have given valuable information about the Party methods—generally working quietly with organizations like the F.B.I. I think the door should always be left open for those who want to return to Americanism.

But when bad records become a virtue, when anybody who claims to have torn up a Communist card is figuratively given king-size keys to the city and permitted publicly to lay about him at honest people—all the while covered by Congressional immunity—I think that's going a bit far.

In the first place, I don't know that all the professional ex-Communists *are* ex-Communists. We've only got their word for it. And unless the Party boys are *complete* dolts it must long ago have occurred to them that some of their number could more effectively do damage and create confusion posing as "former" members.

But suppose, first, that they are all genuinely ex-Communist. Suppose further, that they have been able to throw off the habits of years and are now honest, operating without personal prejudice or regard for publicity and with no ulterior motives at all. Suppose also that they've all suddenly become Really Bright People—which I suspect most Communists are not. There is still the question of how much value to place on testimony about what they heard as Party members.

Even among salesmen in legitimate and successful enterprises there is always the old pep talk and the confidential word about *Yes, sir, just between us, I've practically got old J. Q. Pinchpurse signed up on the dotted line*. And it's not unknown for some publicity agents modestly to take credit for speeches and articles that they had nothing to do with. Well, among the Commies, who are working hard to put across a product that's notably unsuccessful in this country, there must be a good deal of this kind of conversation shoveled around. They've even tried to keep themselves hopped up by

Aug 48

claiming that Jefferson and Lincoln were practically a couple of their boys.

Much of this hearsay testimony seems to me to be at best the recollections of what one trained liar told another trained liar. I don't know why such testimony should be assumed to be infallible and solemnly accepted like stone tablets handed down from a mountain top.

"I Know Leopards—I Used To Be A Leopard Myself"

May 50

When and if these fellows leave the Communist Party, I don't know that they necessarily become towers of strength for the Republic, possessed of omniscience, infallible memories and all the virtues they never had before. I take some of these bleached beets with a few grains of salt.

"How Did Atomic Energy Information Leak Out To The Damn Scientists In The First Place?"

6

The Tsinummoc* Line

THERE IS SO MUCH TALK these days about what Stalin would like, what Stalin would not like, and what would make Stalin happiest of all, that a stranger who came in late might suppose we were all trying to decide what to give a rich uncle for Christmas.

It's not unusual now for a legislator speaking on behalf of some domestic bill to assert knowingly that nothing would make Stalin happier than to see the bill defeated; while an opponent of the bill, speaking with equal authority, insists that nothing would make Stalin happier than to see the same bill passed. If any considerable number of these predictions are accurate, Stalin must certainly be the most mirthful man in the world, shaking like pudding in a vibrating machine, and ready to cry, "Hold! Enough!" just to keep from laughing himself to pieces.

I've drawn a number of smiling Joes in cartoons about policies that might reasonably influence our prospects or Communist chances in the world; and I don't think it's out of place to use Stalin as a symbol of the opposition forces that stand to profit by our mistakes. But that line about what would make him happy keeps bobbing up in speeches and debates on everything from foreign policy to the desirability of building a new comfort station in the local park.

In a real sense anything that contributes to the public welfare may be considered anti-Communist. But there is something sad about this injection of Stalin and Communism into speeches on all subjects. It sounds a little as if the speaker feels obliged to testify that he is in good standing as a patriotic citizen and entitled to have his say, as if he feels that we are so obsessed by a single fear that no other emotion can move us, as if there is something perhaps a little unworthy and suspect about the idea of doing anything right and good and in the public interest just for those reasons alone. These references to Stalin and Communism have become little verbal genuflections, like "if it please the Lord"—but in reverse, of course. And where it used to be said of official follies that the gods must laugh, we now say in one way or another that Stalin smiles.

* Pronounced SIŃ-EW-MOCK, and peddled by political medicine-men.

I'm willing to give the devil his due, but it doesn't seem to me that this dictator belongs in the deity class even in the Powers-of-Darkness department. I just don't think the old boy rates it. He's not that good.

I've never been close enough to the Kremlin to know whether its old walls are rocked by merriment, but I know what makes *me* happy and unhappy. And I'm not cheered by this tendency to consider everything in terms of whether it might please a tyrant. It's possible that he doesn't even know what's good for himself anyhow.

It might be a good idea if all our speakers agreed that what Stalin wants is whatever he can get, and that nothing would make him happier than to see us so fearfully concerned about his pleasure or displeasure that we made complete fools of ourselves. We could let it go at that. I don't have any notion that this will be done but I just toss out the idea as a minor contribution to National Unity.

As a substitute for this preoccupation with Mr. S., perhaps we could hear more in the speeches about what *people* want—people here, people in Europe, in Asia, and in the Middle East—about what would make *them* happy and *us* happy. And if we must consider Stalin in all things, let us visualize him reading the first batch of these public addresses. He glances through them casually at first, then goes over them more intently, following the lines with his finger. When he reaches the end he frowns and turns the pages over to see if there is something on the reverse sides that he has missed; then he thumbs the edges of the pages to see if any are stuck together. He now looks up at a nervous aide, gestures toward the papers, and asks in a hoarse voice, "Where's the rest of it? Where do *I* come in?" The aide, obviously in something of a sweat, explains that this is all there is—the agents went over the complete texts and checked three times. There is nothing more—no references at all to the Great Leader and Hero of His People. Not even much mention of Communism. Just this talk about driving ahead with American programs, world programs, economic and defense programs for the people—always the people.

At this, another aide clears his throat and says, "About all that being-for-the-people stuff, Chief—I think we've got them there. A clear violation of international copyright." But the old man does not answer. He is staring down at the papers and looking a little stunned. These speeches are all wrong. They are downright disrespectful. And worse than that, they give him the feeling that in the struggle for the world he has somehow lost the initiative. Stalin has finally been made unhappy.

The tendency to substitute Old Joe for the Old Nick, and the hastening to justify the most commonplace and necessary items by explaining that they are in some way anti-Communist, might not be of much consequence in itself.

"Couldn't We Make Better Time Driving Forward?"

Mar 47

"Put Me In, Coach! Put Me In!"

Mar 47

But perhaps it is a minor symptom of something that's really dangerous. That is the notion that a purely negative policy of "anti-Communism" can of itself take the place of positive, pro-democratic, pro-people, pro-freedom policies, and—the final delirious twist—the idea that anything the Communists profess to be for we must be against. Pursued to its final illogical conclusion—and some have already arrived there—this means that whenever the Communists claim to be for anything beneficial then we must immediately and automatically be against it.

This business of standing on the head as a substitute for thinking results in quite a rush of blood to the brain and produces some queer viewpoints. One of these was expressed by a spokesman for the real-estate lobby a couple of years ago when he accused Senator Taft of running along with the Communists because the senator advocated a modest amount of public housing. A deadpan examination of his records showed that on a number of occasions his position had indeed paralleled the "Party line," although obviously through no sympathy for Communism. Or, as it used to be put in the election campaigns, he had "voted with Marcantonio." Incidentally, if Marcantonio had been re-elected and if complete opposition to his voting record had become the criterion for electing other congressmen, he might easily have become the most potent man in the legislative body just by the power to administer the kiss of death. And if it became accepted that we must be against anything and everything the Communists profess to be for, of course that pathetic little organ the

"I Don't Know What I'd Do Without You, Mister"

Dec 47

Daily Worker would become the most influential paper in the country. And *must* reading for everybody. How else would you know what to unthink?

This kind of perverted reasoning represents reaction in the literal sense of the word. The people who engage in it are not capable of free-will action but only of *re*action. They are less like men than like mice-in-a-maze, and are bounded by mental iron curtains no less than their Communist counterparts.

May 50

Nov 48

And where the one must learn the Party-line recommendations to know what he is for, the other must study its recommendations just as diligently to find out what he is against.

That sort of thing would put us in the position of an obstinate dog, stubbornly disobeying commands. Beyond the fact that this is hardly a fitting role for the greatest nation in the world, there is the point that a dog which could be counted on to disobey could still be directed. If he could be depended on to go out at the words "Come here" and to stay in at the words "Go out," he would be pretty much under control, even though he might go around laughing fit to kill himself, slapping other dogs on the back and telling them that he's driving the Marster crazy. I think we ought to be a little smarter than that.

When the Communists try to take over the word "democracy," I don't think we need to kiss it a sad good-by. When they pretend to represent liberty we don't need to scuttle the lady with the torch and say, "Nice to have known you." And we don't need to tear up the Bill of Rights because the Communists profess to defend it.

When we can be counted on to oppose anything the Communists say they're for, we will then have the boys in the Kremlin just about where they want us. At this point they will need only to say "Build!" and we will tear down our houses, "Speak!" and we will be dumb, "Breathe!" and we will all automatically clutch our windpipes and drop dead. It may be that each great nation must in time decline and that all the glory of the world must pass, but we don't need to do it to ourselves. And we don't need to let anybody else *make* us do it

Down Stairway

ANTI-COMMUNISM IS THE ONLY ISSUE
FASCISTS ARE PROVEN ANTI-COMMUNISTS
IT'S SAFER TO PLAY BALL WITH FASCISTS THAN WITH DEMOCRATS
DEMOCRACY IS DANGEROUS AND BAD
HERBLOCK
Nov 48

to ourselves. If there is anyone who thinks the Communists do not or would not take full advantage of those who would play this little game of opposites with them, I can only say that he must have more faith in the sincerity and the integrity of the Communists than I have.

There are a number who seem to think that instead of following an American line we should take the Tsinummoc Line—that's *Communist,* of course, spelled backward. Their line has all the same corkscrew twists—in reverse, naturally, but arriving at the same totalitarian end. They would undoubtedly feel happier and safer if we changed the name of Washington, D.C., to Wocsom, and elected as President anybody named Nilats. Then ankle to ankle, men, and backward into the fray!

I don't buy that Tsinummoc line, backward or forward.

This country was not founded on purely negative anti-George-the-Third-ism. If it had been, it would soon have found itself carrying a political line as out of date as cocked hats and powdered wigs and would have been poking around ever since trying to latch on to something else.

The Declaration of Independence started off with an assertion of basic human rights and a concept of what government should be, and then proceeded to measure the rule of George III against them. Those principles are so good and so basic that they provide a measuring stick for all government. The Constitution does not merely say that this is an "anti-monarchy." It carries on the original ideals and puts them into working form. When those documents were drawn up, the course was set for the country and the battle lines were drawn for all the fighting to come.

The course is a straight one, the fight is one fight and always the same fight. Not just anti-monarchy now, anti-emperor another time, anti-Fascist one year, anti-Communist later; not a panicky weaving from side to side and extreme to extreme, perpetually in flight from the claws of God-Knows-What into the jaws of God-Knows-What-Else.

It's the principles of the Declaration and the Bill of Rights against the field. It's democratic freedom against all comers, foreign and domestic, from whatever sides, in whatever combinations, and by whatever labels. It's big enough and strong enough for that. And as long as we know that it's one fight and remember what that fight is, we'll always win. Because it's the fight of all the people of the world.

It's nice to know where you want to go and to head straight for it. You don't have to zig then because somebody says "Zag!" or zag because somebody else says "Zig!" You don't have to drive your car into a ditch every time somebody else hauls out a road map and hints he might go a piece in the same direction. You don't have to follow a tortuous, twisting line—forward or in reverse.

And you don't get dizzy going around the curves.

7

Not Entirely Foreign

SOONER OR LATER foreign policy always comes up; and in the middle of an interesting dinner discussion about Miss Galvanized Pail of 1952 you're likely to find that the whole conversation has suddenly gone abroad and all the guests are pitched for battle without anyone even having blown a whistle. Hardly anybody who *is* anybody around here would be seen in public any more without a foreign policy, and some of our more prominent senators have a different one for every day of the week.

If a senator is *very* prominent and finds that his office is so cluttered with his old foreign policies that he keeps tripping over them, he can weed out some of his more obvious boners—which can be carted off to the incinerator in a couple of medium-size trucks—and bundle off the rest of them to a publisher. Presented between hard covers and offered with a straight face, these can be passed off just as if they comprised a consistent and sensible policy—particularly if they are given a good solid title like *A Former Policy for Americans* or *Wait—I Think I've Got It This Time.* This may not straighten out the politician's record, but it at least helps to straighten out his office, and makes room for new campaign literature about his braininess and integrity.

Up to now I've never been a collector of anything much except old newspapers, and this is only inadvertent because I can't remember what it was I was going to clip out of them. But lately I've been tempted to start collecting foreign policies. Of course, I couldn't keep up with all the latest issues of these policies, but I could specialize in those of a few individuals, and maybe could team up with somebody who saves old campaign buttons to exhibit both collections together.

The approach to foreign affairs is interesting enough in itself. I've met some students of the subject who speak of it almost mystically. To a few of them statecraft is evidently a kind of witchcraft that a select priesthood is privileged to practice, and you wouldn't understand it, old boy. Sometimes if you lean forward slightly as they murmur the words, "foreign affairs," you can hear little chimes bonging inside their heads.

There is another group that also practices Mumbo-Jumbo in this field but disguises its formula as *anti*-Mumbo-Jumbo. These people represent what might be called the bruiser approach, and their idea of the way to meet all international situations is to poke an elbow into somebody's ribs and assert, "I'm an Ammurican, bud, y'unnerstand?" And they might add, "Tell those Communists in China to go back where they came from, see?" in the same way they'd tell a waiter to take back the soup. To them anything else is "striped-pants diplomacy" practiced by "cookie-pushers."

I don't think it's necessary to put on a tall pointed cap and take a sorcerer's apprenticeship to deal with our world neighbors. And I don't think either that any American boy in white flannels can send villains scurrying and set the people of foreign lands into quaint native dances just by looking clean-cut and drawing the Stars and Stripes from his breast pocket.

To begin with, "foreign" and "domestic" policies can't be completely separated, corked up, and labeled like bottles of wine. They're all in one barrel, and whatever policy there is has to be big enough to cover the works.

With the weight we've taken on in the world in recent years, sometimes we don't know our own strength. Nevertheless, there's hardly anything that goes on here any more that doesn't get some kind of a play-back abroad—including speeches that politicians turn out purely for home consumption. They blow in here and it comes out there. Our domestic policies come out there too.

When inflation runs loose in this country it's not just a little family joke on the American consumer. It also cuts into the purchasing power of other countries who buy from us and borrow from us—*and for heaven's sake, what did*

Mar 47

"Atom Bombs Ain't The Only Explosives"

May 51

they do with that money we loaned them LAST *year?* Congressmen may pass a bill to cut down our imports of a few products just as a friendly favor to some special-interest group at home. But if the countries that depend on selling us those products start turning red under the collar or blue around the fingernails, these same congressmen are likely to regard this as a "foreign" problem—

"Say, You're In A Tough Spot There"

Jun 47

and what's the matter with those crazy people over there? Why doesn't our State Department or somebody DO *something about that situation?*

In the postwar cartoons that serve as lantern slides for this travelogue, there are a couple on the Information Program, including the Voice of America, which was set up in 1947. If you've glanced at these cartoons, it will come as no surprise to learn that I think this program has been worth its moderate cost. But I don't think we can expect miracles just because the people abroad hear a Voice. They hear lots of voices, many of them from this country, which say a lot of different things. We can't synchronize them as totalitarians do—and we don't want to—but there ought to be some relationship between words and deeds. I think we ought to be able to have a Voice that can speak up real plain for democratic principles without having congressmen at its throat. As they say in domestic political campaigns, you can't beat something with nothing. If our government can only say, "Yah yah yah, Communism is no good!" that may sound to people in other countries very much like, "Yah yah yah, Americanism is no good!" And in this kind of a contest the Kremlin might even have a little the edge on us because that's their specialty.

What that Kremlin crowd was up to in the spring of '47 is also illustrated in some of these drawings. The one of Gromyko and the bomb was done when they rejected proposals for atomic control. In those days they didn't say—as Vishinsky did in 1951—that the proposals kept them laughing all night, but they were terribly worried that such plans would interfere with national

Penny Whistle

May 49

"The Gasp You Just Heard Was The Voice Of America"

Jun 47

"You Tell 'Em, Kid—I'm A Sovereign Power Myself"

Mar 47

"What Are You Doing After The Trial, Baby?"

Apr 47

sovereignty. Soviet national sovereignty, that is. Not Czechoslovakian, for example. Nor Polish. Nor Lithuanian. Nor Bulgarian. Nor Rumanian. Nor Hungarian.

The Foot Is Familiar

Feb 48

"You Want The Police? I'm The Police"

Feb 48

The Czech coup occurred about a year later and happened so fast that I had to draw two cartoons the same day—the one of the foot in the door, which appeared in the early edition, being replaced by the one of the hand at the throat in later editions. The cartoon of the Soviet "farewell" in North Korea also appeared in 1948 and remained timely a lot longer.

The drawing of Molotov chucking Germany under the chin was done during the Big Four foreign ministers' meeting in Moscow—as was the ballet cartoon. The latter brought me a letter from one reader expressing shock that I had pictured Secretary Marshall in such an undignified manner. But I later learned that a clipping of the cartoon had been forwarded to him along with more important papers, and that it had given him one of the few laughs he got out of the whole frustrating trip. There was, of course, no occasion for my correspondent to be shocked by the cartoon picturization of an eminent public figure in tights. But I wish now that I'd saved that letter just as a memento of happier days before McCarthyism and Communism had slung their mud at men like Marshall, brought national and international politics to the gutter level, and reduced our sensibilities to near numbness.

The Marshall Plan was conceived later in 1947, and was approved by Congress in 1948, largely because of the leadership of Senator Vandenberg. It has been called one of the great victories of peace, but this victory wasn't achieved without some pretty persistent attempts to kick it away. Some obstructionists in Congress worked hard to whittle the plan down to ineffective-

Parting Is Such Sweet Sorrow

Sep 48

Ballet In Moscow

Apr 47

May 47 *May 48*

ness, but the Moscow team was not to be outdumb by anybody; and when it pulled itself and its satellites out of the early Marshall Plan discussions it practically insured passage of the measure.

I probably shouldn't speak of obstructionists. Nobody is an obstructionist any more—or an isolationist. They may look as if they are; they may talk as if they are; they may act as if they are. But they're not. They're simply legislators who believe firmly in economy, which is a noble aim. Not economy on pork-barrel legislation, of course, or on other things where money can be saved effectively—just economy on the things that really win for us, economy where economy comes high. Those great thrifty souls exemplified in the "Counting the Gains" cartoon are nonetheless vigorously anti-Communist in their public addresses, which cost nothing and are frequently worth it. If totalitarianism could be smothered under a stack of speeches, these staunch fellows would be our first line of defense.

For the busy reader who hasn't had time to investigate the various foreign policies that are currently being peddled at other counters, I'll give a brief digest of a couple of the more popular items, one of which is just such an "economy" policy. This one advocates sitting on the back porch and rocking back and forth vigorously. It is for curtailing our foreign programs, staying home, sneering at the United Nations, and at the same time hurling back Communism on all fronts. This is to be accomplished at minimum cost by hiring a small boy who will hide under the desk of the Secretary of State, wait till Joe Stalin turns up in one of the drawers, and then fell him with a pea shooter. It is a basic assumption of this policy that Stalin *is* in one of those desk drawers, which conveniently fits in with the idea that we need to do little abroad. This policy can also be used to rub into your scalp, where it will cure dandruff by removing the scalp completely.

There is another policy, which can be purchased separately or in combination with this one, that proclaims itself, out of the side of its mouth, to be anti-idealistic. The label says it is full of "realism" and "national self-interest," and the ads sometimes mention "balance of power." The general theory of this one seems to be that anything which makes sense can't be clever enough; and anything which helps others must be bad for us. This anti-idealism stuff is so realistic that it only requires turning back the clocks a few centuries. Along with this policy, which can be either taken intravenously or smoked in a pipe, comes a full-size mallet for beating ourselves about the ears to show how hard-headed we are, and—listen, boys and girls—a *realistic* simulated-gold poison ring with a secret code inside. Only you and the other boys and girls who have these secret rings will be able to understand policy or be able to slip knockout drops into your little friends' milkshakes.

By now I'm fed up to here with the kind of talk about "national self-interest," which seems to imply that any policies that don't kick our neighbors in the teeth must be for selling our country down the river. *All* foreign policies —unless they're proposed by people who are literally traitors—are designed

"We've Got To Cut Wherever We Can"

Jan 48

"Aren't There Certain Risks Involved In Boating?"

May 48

for national self-interest. The only difference is that one type is more successful than another.

We had some fine examples of "economy" and "hard-headed practical self-interest" in the twenties—followed closely by a nice economic world depression and a good hard-headed world war. And they both cost us plenty. After World War II we had the Marshall Plan which helped to save Europe for democracy; and, among other types of foreign aid, a food program which

"Shall We Say Grace?"

Oct 47

"Make Any Discoveries?"

Oct 47

"See Any Short Cut?"

Nov 47

was based on the notion that we'd better not let the people of Europe starve. The voluntary sacrifices which this program asked of us would hardly be visible under the Palomar lens, but the effects abroad were important. I did a series of food cartoons during that period, and the "Shall We Say Grace" drawing was, from the standpoint of special reprints, as popular as any in this book. A great many of the requests came from churches—which have been trying to tell us for a good many years now that idealism and aid to others are not necessarily impractical.

When the Marshall Plan and the food programs were under discussion, several congressmen went abroad to look over the situation. These were legitimate investigations. I've done cartoons kidding other congressional trips which were obviously junkets, but I'm reluctant to condemn them as a waste of taxpayers' money. I think it's a good idea for congressmen to get around and see the world. But I think also that a person who sets foot on foreign soil doesn't necessarily absorb knowledge about the area through the soles of his shoes. A little travel can be a dangerous thing, if it provides only a partial picture which is misleading—or if a congressman gets a few labels pasted onto his luggage only so that he can paste on to his preconceived opinions the tag-line "I was *there!*" In the fable of the blind men and the elephant, each of the blind men was *there* all right, but all of them might have got a more accurate idea of the situation by staying home and listening to the reports of better observers.

Well, that question of the value of congressional junkets is one that I wrestle with in a mild sort of way each year when they take off for foreign

"One Day Last Week We Had An Egg"

Nov 47

"I Don't See Anybody That Looks Undernourished"

Oct 47

parts. I think most of them learn something on these journeys, some of them learn a great deal; and the only times I really begrudge any of them the trips are those occasions when an inevitable few go a long way from home to make asses of themselves.

Congressman Taber, a great "economy" advocate, returned from his post-

"You Looking For A Communist Organizer, Mister?"

Mar 47

"How Much A Pound Are You Worth?"

Oct 47

"Save The Holy Places"

Apr 48

"We Want To Make Our Position Perfectly Clear—"

Apr 48

war tour to say that he had seen no signs of undernourishment abroad—though more thorough and more competent observers had seen an alarming amount of it. This prompted the drawing of him looking into the mirror. That one was a little tough and it was meant to be.

The next exhibits in this travel talk are a couple on the Palestine situation

Gandhi

Jan 31, 48—On the death of Gandhi

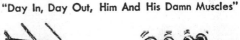

"Day In, Day Out, Him And His Damn Muscles"

Oct 48

in 1948, and I'm conscious of the fact that they don't show our brightest hours or tell a complete story. That, again, is because cartoons are designed to provide a kick in the pants rather than to record happy endings. So in a combination of drawings like this, I'm left, you might say, without a third act.

It seemed to me that the creation of the Israeli democracy had an importance that could not be measured in oil drums, and these cartoons represented the way I felt about a temporarily upside-down U.S. policy which was supposed to be based on strategy—and which the strategists later conceded had been wrong. As usual, the cartoons stopped when the issue was settled. But—hooking around my ears the whiskers of history and whipping out a long quill pen—I can at least record here that U.S. policy did a final flip-flop and our government was the first to extend recognition to the new country.

There are those who think it's silly, visionary, and wasteful to promote democracy in the world, to go about making friends, and to help make those friends strong. Still, there's a little something to be said for policies like that. They happen to be the ones that work.

'Now, If You'd Like To See Something In A Larger Book—'

Nov 47

8

Late Returns

IN THE POLITICAL-OBSERVATION BUSINESS nothing can take the place of a survey in which you get around and meet people and set down opinions. I've been conducting one of these exhaustive surveys, and since I get exhausted pretty easily in election years, it didn't take very long. I must have talked to upward of half a dozen people, not counting the ones I set down as "Don't Know." The latter included a barber who kept interrupting me to tell me what *he* thought, and an old gentleman who turned off his hearing aid just when I was getting up a good head of steam. As a result of these efforts I can now make some observations which would otherwise have been made without talking to anybody at all.

Our national-election politics is often referred to as a "great game," but that's an understatement. Actually, it's our Number One spectator sport and something of a substitute for a national sweepstakes. Only half of us may be interested in government enough to vote, but everybody speculates about who might be elected; and the saying that "any American boy can become President" is partly a reflection of the national interest in jackpots.

What everybody's really interested in is: Who will win the Big Prize? And the winner hardly has a chance to warm the executive seat before we're off again, speculating on who'll be the *next* one—and whether the current winner wants to try for double. Since the passage of the Twenty-second Amendment, a President can no longer try for more than double because many people feared that this might tend to cut down the number of contestants and spoil the fun.

What we expect of a President—or rather what the political wiseacres *expect* us to expect of one—is simple:

He must be able to knock off for himself the biggest political job in the world, but he must not be a "politician." He must be a man who can bring about complete unity, and he must take a courageous and forthright stand on all issues. He must be Superman but, of course, just a regular average guy. And his candidacy must be in reluctant response to a popular demand—even if he has had to stump every county in the country to create it.

There ain't no such animal. But there is a whole mythology of this sort of stuff about what a candidate should be, how he should behave, what's proper and what's taboo. I look forward to the time when a candidate, invited to pose catching a fish, will announce clearly and distinctly that he *hates* fishing and is going around the corner to shoot a game of kelly pool. On the basis of a five-second survey of my typewriter, I figure that the result of such unorthodox behavior would be as follows:

Political advisers stricken with apoplexy	6
Editorials citing the candidate as a bad example to the Nation's youth (published in newspapers that are against him anyhow)	36
Editorials commending the candidate for his courage, integrity, and honesty (published in newspapers that are for him anyhow)	36
Votes lost	10
Votes gained	12
Total	100

Our political rituals have already begun to flake a little around the edges, particularly since the trend away from formal notifications of the party nominees. These always used to be good for a few cartoons showing the members of a notification delegation, some weeks after the close of the conventions, winking and nudging each other as they surprised the winning candidate with the news of his nomination.

In 1948 President Truman followed the precedent-breaking precedent begun by Franklin D. Roosevelt in 1932, of accepting the nomination right at the convention hall, and making no secret of the fact that he had heard the

"Cannon To Right Of Them, Cannon To Left Of Them"

"We Now Return You To Washington"

Feb 48

Jul 48

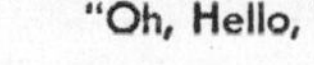

"This Is A Far, Far Better Thing You Do—"

Dec 47

"Oh, Hello, Tom—I Thought It Was The Secret Service"

Sep 48

news. Mr. Truman, just for good measure, announced also that he was calling a special session of Congress. This occasioned the cartoon "We Now Return You to Washington," as well as some editorial eyebrow-raising because he had made this announcement at a political gathering.

The eyebrows stayed up throughout his "give-'em-hell" campaign and right

The Big Train

Nov 48

"Now, About Predictions For Next Year—"

Dec 48

"Next Stop, Wyoming—9 Votes"

July 47

July 47

up to the day of the election. It is an unwritten law that election-eve statement must be dignified and non-political. But on the evening of November 1, 1948 there was a final touch of Harry in the night when he told the people to "Vot tomorrow—Vote Democratic." Twenty-four million of them did, and anothe political tradition bit the dust.

In 1952 the Republicans nominated a Presidential candidate who did no openly campaign for the nomination till late in the season; and the Demo crats chose a man who had not sought the honor at all. But the pre-conven tion behavior of most candidates follows pretty much of a fixed pattern, sim ilar to that of male birds that go into a pre-courtship routine of struttin around, displaying their plumage, whistling to themselves, and pretendin they're just out for a walk.

The political early birds usually take trips around the country just to se how things are going, make a few talks here and there, shake hands, and cha with other politicians. Nobody but a cad would suggest that this is campaign ing. I'm a cad, by the way.

"The office seeks the man," but naturally anybody with a high regard fo that office doesn't want to see it stumbling around in the wrong directio meeting up with the wrong fellows.

After the candidates have flushed themselves into the open, they then ge into the state Presidential-primary business, which is a mess.

Fewer than half the states hold Presidential primaries, and each has its ow special rules about who and what the voter may cast his ballot for, and what the vote means, if anything.

The Eisenhower candidacy brought out the additional peculiarities of state primaries regarding write-in votes. In one state a nickname like "Ike" may be acceptable, while another state may count only those write-ins in which the full name of the candidate is neatly printed with a ballpoint pen while the voter is submerged under water.

It is not generally considered good etiquette or discreet strategy for one candidate to enter the primary in another's home state. Mr. Harold Stassen, a career Presidential candidate, tossed this tradition out the window when he entered the Ohio primary against Senator Taft in 1948. The firehouse cartoon was drawn at this time, and the adjoining cartoon came in 1952 when Mr. Stassen was cooled off in his own state.

Uniform Presidential primaries held throughout the entire country would give all the voters a direct say about which candidates the parties should nominate. On such a scale they might also make physical wrecks of the candidates, but this is something of an occupational hazard even under the present method.

Such a primary system might also help to simplify the work of the political conventions, leaving more time for working on party platforms and for preparing the spontaneous demonstrations. But while this might eliminate some polling of delegations on the first ballot, it would not do away with conven-

"To Hell With The Cornfields! Save The Fire House!"

Apr 48

Springtime In Minnesota

Mar 52

tional nominating routine unless one candidate managed to round up a majority of delegates in the primaries.

I usually go to the conventions, where I try to look like a working newspaperman and am generally allotted an impressive badge that says "Usher," or sometimes "Alternate Messenger." This entitles me to be told that I'm sit-

"Yes Suh, He's A Real Sho Nuff Ol' Houn' Dawg"

Oct 48

ting in the wrong seat, bud; and also gives me full privileges to sweat through the hot speeches, get trampled in the general crush, and return home bruised and beaten, just the same as anyone else. It also gives me an opportunity to talk with other newspapermen that I haven't seen since the last convention. We ask each other, "What do you think?" wag our heads, make clucking

Jun 52 *Mar 52*

noises, and exchange opinions—which turn out to be the same ones that are available in all the newspapers.

Party platforms come in for a lot of gags about not meaning anything. The catch on party platforms and the reason they come in for so many gags is that they aren't particularly binding on anybody. Even the party nom-

Jun 52—before the keynote speech . . . and *after* *Jul 52*

"—And Now Here Comes Another Delegate—"

Jul 52

"Very Interesting And Educational"

Jul 52

inees can pretend they weren't listening when the platform was adopted, and the Congressional candidates go their own ways anyhow. On the national and state tickets the slogan is "All together, fellows—every man for himself."

There is no more touching example of unity than that of a couple of candidates on a party ticket smilingly standing arm in arm before the cameras

"What Do You Mean What Program Am I Listening To?"

Jul 52

Jul 52

"I've Always Said You Were A Great Guy"

Jul 52

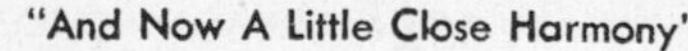
"And Now A Little Close Harmony"

Jul 52

and each wishing the other would drop dead. And there was no better example of the actualities of party politics than the 1952 pre-primary contest in Texas, in which two Democratic senatorial candidates vied with each other in telling the voters how much they opposed the policies of the President—who also happened to be a Democrat.

Since the local political situations are so important, I might as well men-

"But If You Want A Hot Accompanist—"

May 52

"Gee—Ain't He Terrific!"

Jul 52

"There Must Be Some Better Way To Do This"

Jul 52

"Who Do You Think You'll Vote Against?"

Mar 48

tion a couple of points of Standard Operating Procedure regarding outside aid in local elections. If you are a candidate for office, the money and aid you receive from outside your own state show that you are a National Figure. that the Country Needs You, and that the People of America Are Rallying to You. The aid contributed to your opponent's campaign from outside the local area shows the influence of Carpetbaggers, Interfering With the Conduct of Our Affairs, and Trying to Tell the People of Our Great State How to Vote.

Every state, is, of course, a Great State. It is a wonderful experience to go through a convention or a campaign listening to speech after speech—and realizing, as you drift into unconsciousness, that there is not a locality in the entire broad country that is anything less than Great and that does not in its own special way help to form Men of Great Character.

After all the Men of Great Character from all the Great States have finally nominated the Greatest Men of All, the conventions are then adjourned and are followed by One of the Dirtiest Campaigns in American History.

I don't know how many votes are won during a campaign—or how many are lost because voters listen to one side and then run to vote for the other.

During political campaigns I'm frequently told, "You must be having a picnic with so much political stuff to work on." And it *is* fun. The only drawback is that feelings get to running so high that any drawing of a candidate which does not show him embodying the virtues of Washington, Jefferson, and Lincoln will be regarded by some of his supporters as a dastardly act.

In 1952 the nominations of Governor Stevenson and General Eisenhower gave the voters—and the cartoonists—two new faces in a Presidential election for the first time in twenty-four years. On whatever basis people made up their minds about these new national political figures, the cartoon of the two men on the streetcar illustrates a feeling I've had for some time about the way we often vote. When I say "for some time," that's not just a figure of speech. I did one version of this cartoon in 1932 and recall it well because I had to argue with an editor to retain the word *who* in the title instead of substituting the grammatically correct *whom*. In the spring of 1948 I jacked up the title and ran a new drawing under it; and the cartoon was later re-issued in the spring of 1952.

The extra mileage I've had out of that cartoon, however, has been nothing compared to that which politicians have got out of some of *their* election-year stuff. There's one pair of campaign arguments that leaves me cold to the point of putting on earmuffs. One side of this corn is the argument that a party or an incumbent should be re-elected simply by virtue of being already in office—because of experience or because if you swap horses in the middle of the stream you'll rock the boat. If we took that one seriously it would mean that any person or party elected to office should remain with it till death or impeachment did them part. Which is obviously silly.

The argument on the other side, which also strikes me with the force of a damp feather, is that the "out" candidate or party should be elected because

"I Have The Same Trouble"

Jan 52

"Haw, Haw, Haw!—Ooops!"

Apr 52

of having been "out" for a while. The clincher on this argument is that we must do this "to preserve the two-party system"—and a soggier punch line I've never heard.

It's not the people's job to keep a political party in business. It's the political party's job to keep itself in business by offering policies and candidates that meet the needs and wants of the people. When one party can no longer do that it's replaced by another—as the Republican party came up when the Whig party knocked itself out; or else the party in office eventually splits itself in two—which is very nearly what the Democratic party did between 1932 and 1952. Since the Democrats and Republicans are both pretty well divided among themselves, the argument—which has no validity in any case—might as well be that we should vote to preserve the four-party system.

In the 72-year period between 1860 and 1932, the Democrats were able to elect only two Presidents, whose combined terms in office totaled just sixteen years. But our political system did not go up in smoke. And neither, for that matter, did the Democratic Party.

Predictions are a big item in any campaign and total almost as many words as the election post-mortems. We all want to be "in the know," and this sometimes leads to an affliction that might be called "inside-dopiness." I don't refer to the ferreting out of genuine information, but to the unquestioning acceptance of any prediction that's repeated often enough, of any collection of potato peelings, old tin cans, and grapefruit rinds that's labeled "confidential," and of any private statement that's heard from some Big Wheel *himself*—even though there may be a hundred items on the public record to refute it. I think there's such a thing as getting so deep inside the horse's mouth that you can't see what's going on.

Thanks largely to the opinion polls and the hypnotic effect of prognosticators on each other, it was possible in 1948 for almost everybody to have access to the wrong result in advance. There was enough inside dope around to stuff an elephant—which is very nearly what it did.

As columnist Bill Gold observed in the summer of that year, "All the polls and predictions may be right and the outcome may be 99 per cent certain. But they're still going ahead and having the election, aren't they?"

There is, of course, always the final question of whether the Electoral College will come creaking through to confirm the people's choice. It hasn't always done this, and various proposals have been made for altering the Electoral College system. There is one way to make sure that the popular vote prevails. That is to abolish the Electoral College and simply leave the election of Presidents to the direct vote of the people. This would be a very sensible change and of course it is not likely to be adopted.

Probably the most cogent statement on elections was made by Winston Churchill, who has had some little experience in this field. He once remarked that elections are always bad and that the only thing worse would be not having them.

"Don't Expect Me To Get This Real Accurate, Bub"

Oct 48

9

Who's Representing Who?

I DON'T KNOW how it is now, but when I started to school there was a lot of reciting of the Preamble to the Constitution. And when we came to the phrase, "we do ordain and establish this constitution," I spoke the line doggedly and with some small clenching of the fists, under the impression that the words *do ordain* were some kind of variation of *do-or-die*. And if there was anybody around who had any idea of trying to stop us from establishing this Constitution for the United States, he was going to have to do it over my prone form.

A little grammar and elementary history cleared up that misapprehension, but a little more grammar had me wondering about a couple of other words in that same Preamble. These are the ones which refer to the forming of a "more perfect" union. Obviously a thing is either perfect or it isn't, and if it's perfect how can it be more so? Maybe this is one of those things like Shakespeare's "most unkindest cut of all," which was evidently correct in its time, or perhaps it's one of those word combinations that conventions sometimes paste together in an effort to please everyone.

What started me thinking about all this is that I want to say something about the representation in that union, and it would sound nice if I said it ought to be "more perfect." But that wouldn't be accurate, even though it might satisfy our Communists-in-Reverse who think we're giving aid and comfort to the enemy by admitting anything less than perfection. That, incidentally, is a typically totalitarian notion; and I think most people sense the fact that any government that has to put on such a pose must have a lot more wrong with it than most governments. The Soviet claims of perfection must hand a particularly big laugh to people who have lived under other dictatorships that made the same kind of claim and also shut up anybody who thought differently. The best part of our system is that the things that are wrong with it are never so bad that they can't be discussed, debated, even advertised to the world—and corrected.

Well, what I want to talk about is not the exercise of our civil rights, or that annual lynching which the Commies are always dusting off and propping up for propaganda purposes—but the way our representative system is working, just on a population basis. I have a special interest in this subject because as a resident of the District of Columbia I don't have any representation at all. Not anywhere.

Occasionally I do a cartoon like the one of Congress and the baby, but I'm not sure that most people outside the Capital understand that there is in the United States a city of 800,000 people where no elections of any kind are held. It's so, and I'm one of the politically underprivileged who live there. Some people go to Paris and lose their hearts. I came to Washington and lost my vote.

"Honestly, I'd Rather Walk"

May 50

You sometimes hear a man say that he wouldn't vote for this person or that person for dog-catcher. This is pretty academic because even back home in Illinois, in the days when I could cast a ballot, I don't remember ever seeing candidates for dog-catcher listed. But if dog-catchers *were* elected, we Washingtonians wouldn't even have the opportunity of *not* voting for them. An estimated third of the people here probably have been able to maintain voting rights somewhere else. But the rest of us can't vote for President, senator, congressman, mayor, sheriff, councilman, or anything. If the police department here were made up entirely of thieves we couldn't do much about it. What I mean, we have no voice in government, national or local—no vote of any kind at all. We don't even get a chance to go through the motions of saying "Ja," "Nein," "Da," or "Nyet." We are wards of the U.S. Congress.

Of course we're not completely without privileges. We are allowed to pay taxes, both federal and local. In fact, the government is so anxious to make us feel almost like regular citizens that it rather insists on our paying these. You know what taxation without representation is. I'm not one to incite lawlessness, but I sometimes wonder what would happen if the few hundred thousand of us who live here simply neglected to pay any taxes until we got the rights of American citizens. From time to time there's talk of dressing up as Indians and dumping tea into the Potomac harbor, but this idea probably would be too subtle to impress Congress.

If anyone thinks that we show a lack of proper respect for U.S. congressmen here, please remember that to us in Washington these fellows, by their own desire and through no choice of ours, are just local councilmen. They decide, through weary hours of debate, whether we should be allowed to have daylight saving time, how high our weeds should be allowed to grow, and what size fish should be sold in our local markets. We are a great and unwilling burden upon them, but they bear up, even though they have to neglect the nation's business to argue about our local problems. Nothing is too much trouble to keep democracy out of the nation's Capital. A couple of years ago when Congress, in a captious moment, passed a resolution in favor of a united Ireland, I did a cartoon suggesting that the Irish parliament might go on record in favor of home rule for the District of Columbia. It seemed only appropriate.

But about the country in general—about representation for those lucky people who have the franchise:

It's sometimes said that we Americans get the kind of government we deserve. This certainly is true of the 50 per cent or so who don't take the trouble to vote, but I don't think the other half is getting full weight.

The horse-and-rabbit-stew cartoon—based on the old gag about the cook

"Don't Bother Me—I've Got Smaller Fish To Fry"

Jul 51

"You Mean Some Can And Don't Do It?"

Oct 50

who made such a dish out of "equal parts": one horse and one rabbit—illustrates a certain defect in our representation. This involves a little arithmetic, but not much. U.S. Congressional districts are supposed to contain approximately equal numbers of voters, to insure equal representation. But the 1950 census showed that in one state alone the differences in population between

Horse-And-Rabbit Stew

Feb 51

"It's A Crime How Those Big City Machines Operate"

Aug 51

one district and another ran as high as 700,000. Every voter might be said to have a congressman, but it's not hard to see that the people of one of these areas had about eight times as much representation in Washington as the other. If 167,000 voters are entitled to one representative, 908,000 voters should be entitled to five or six of them. Right?

These mathematical tricks generally favor the rural areas. The state legislatures are responsible for this because they lay out the voting districts. The legislatures are generally under rural control because the rural voters originally outnumbered the urban ones. And the legislators, not wishing to redistrict themselves out of power or out of office, simply did a Rip Van Winkle on population shifts and kept the voting districts as nearly as possible the way they had been in the good old days. The same system was followed in laying out the U.S. Congressional districts within the states, so that the city areas often are short-changed on representation in Washington as well as in the state capitals.

In 1951 several legislatures reduced some of the more glaring inequalities; but even when the population difference in districts has been narrowed down to 250,000 in one as against 500,000 in another, one group of voters obviously is still getting twice as much representation as another. In one of the state governments where reapportionment was being debated in 1951, a legislator stated frankly that the rural voters should continue to get more than their share of representation because they were "more stable." That's an interesting theory of government, but it's not what the framers of the Constitution had in mind.

This is not a reflection on rural residents. I think each of them is entitled to the same representation as anyone else. In the tractor cartoon, please note that the driver is not a farmer but a "farm politician," and beneath the overalls he wears a business suit.

Unequal representation is not new and it rates only occasional articles in the papers, generally during census years. But I think it's worth more notice —because our whole system of government depends on fair elections. One effect of this kind of representation run-around is that it helps to elect Congresses which lack sufficient interest in things such as the urban consumers' desire for price controls. If you think you're gypped at the market, it may go back to the fact that some state legislators have their heavy thumbs on the scales of government.

Item 2 on representation: A section of the Fourteenth Amendment provides that any state which limits the voting rights of its citizens shall have its representation in Congress reduced proportionately. So that if a state which hangs a "Restricted" sign on the ballot box allows only half of its population to vote, it's supposed to have 50 per cent fewer congressmen. Of course this amendment is not enforced—despite the fact that congressmen take an oath to uphold the Constitution—and so our national representation is thrown that much more out of balance.

So much for the states. In Washington, the will of the majority comes up against another obstacle course. It first runs into the long white whiskers of

"It's A Hell Of A Way To Run A Railroad"

Nov 48

the Congressional seniority system, pictured in the cartoon of the trainmen. This is the age-before-duty code by which Congress rewards with important committee posts some of its members who have given it the best years of their lives—frequently after those best years are over.

The seniority system may be great for veteran employees, lodge officers, and old beaux, but it has its drawbacks in democratic government. The theory of this line-of-succession system is that when a man has been elected to several consecutive terms in Congress he must have plenty on the ball. But it ain't necessarily so. Some of them have been able to sign long-term leases here because they come from what are called "safe" districts—which is to say, safely in a political rut, safely unrepresentative, or safely under the control of a well-oiled machine.

This may be a little beside the point, but it seems to me that there is a kind of perverted native pride which also operates for congressmen who can grab enough headlines to make themselves well known even if not favorably known. Some voters seem to feel, like the politician who supported a notably bad candidate of his party, that, "after all, he's *our* s.o.b.!" Or it may be due simply to the value of repetition in advertising that these voters make their X before any name that rings a bell in their minds, even though the bell is a warning gong.

At any rate, re-election isn't exactly synonymous with statesmanship. A community just beyond Al Capp's Dogpatch might be strong for the most isolationist man in the whole isolated area, but a dozen terms from that district wouldn't make him the ideal man to be chairman of the Foreign Affairs Committee of the U.S. Congress.

In the Eighty-second Congress, Senator McCarran, chairman of the Senate Judiciary Committee, represented fewer constituents than almost any other member of either house of Congress. Senator McKellar, chairman of the Senate Appropriations Committee, had been elected to six terms with the aid of Boss Crump's machine. The heads of committees like these exercise a lot of power over legislation. They hold those positions not through outstanding ability, not by the will of the American people or of their senators, not even by the confidence of their fellow party members—but by the Divine Right of Seniority. It's not *impossible* for good men to come to the top through this system, and some do—but this obviously isn't the way to insure getting them.

Presidential "trouble with Congress" is an old story, and there have always been conflicts between the two branches. But the stacking of Congressional districts and the power of a few men to obstruct the Congresses that *are* elected contribute their part to deadlock government. The fact is that, whomever they cast their ballots for, the voters can't be sure of getting a Congress

Fruits Of Victory

"Father, Dear Father—"

Mar 49

Feb 50

that will co-operate fully with any President of either party. That's the way it stacks up. The promotion of party responsibility in an administration is enough reason for dumping the seniority system. But most members of the Senate and the House evidently feel that they are already on the way up the seniority ladder and thus have a vested interest in the system. As they continue to sit in Congress the vests and the interests expand together. So, as each of Napoleon's soldiers figuratively carried a marshal's baton in his knapsack, every legislator carries a chairman's gavel in his briefcase. It's a tough system to break.

But this isn't all. Each branch of Congress has its own gimmick for tying things up a little tighter. In the Senate it's the filibuster.

This is frankly a device for frustrating the majority will, and even the threat of it is generally enough to send legislation quivering back into a pigeonhole. When one of those Big Blows takes place, the "greatest deliberative body in the world" is engaged in a physical endurance contest in which brains are less important than strong lungs, legs, and kidneys. When the majority tries to break a filibuster by calling for all-night sessions, it's also important to be able to continue standing and talking while in a state of semiconsciousness—an ability which some have developed to a remarkable degree, possibly from practice at regular sessions and at Washington cocktail parties.

Feats of endurance are fine for the Olympics, but they don't provide the best way of settling issues in the U.S. Senate. The gag cartoon illustrates the cry of the filibusterers that they are being deprived of their rights if they

"No Fair Trying To Gag Me"

"Want To Borrow A Corkscrew, Suh, You-All?"

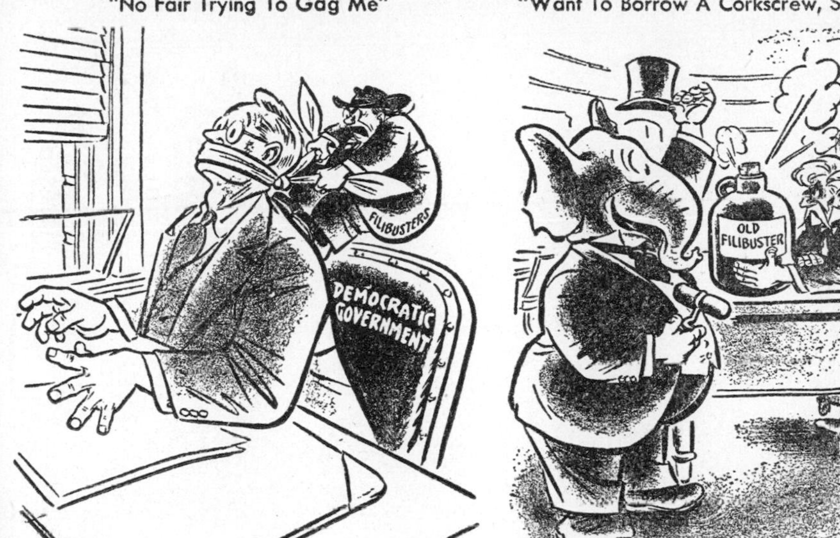

Jan 49

Jul 48

cannot indefinitely obstruct the majority. That's quite a gag indeed. Of course the difficulty in ending this minority veto power is that a move to change the rules on filibusters during a session can itself be filibustered.

There is no unlimited debate (*translation:* filibuster) in the House of Representatives. But that body has its own self-imposed chains to hinder legislative progress. It gives its Rules Committee the power to smother bills approved

"Scram! We Got Too Many People That Believe In Democracy Already!"

"I Got No Control Over Myself"

Feb 50

Jan 46

"Come In—Come In"

Feb 51

"There Must Be Some Better Way We Can Run This"

Jan 50

by other committees. The House ended this tyranny for one session, 1949–50; but it couldn't stand the freedom, and in 1951 asked to have the leg irons slipped back on again. Then why, as they ask in the textbooks, are congressmen willing to submit like this? One reason is that the Rules Committee's power provides a convenient out for legislators who want to see bills killed off but don't want the blame for having done the hatchet job. They can appear to support bills which they know the committee will put out of the way, then rattle their chains before the voters and say, "You see? We were helpless."

Actually there's never a time when a majority of the House can't put through a bill if it's willing to get tough enough. It can force a measure to the floor by petition if it really wants to—but it hardly ever wants to.

Corruption and subversion get a lot of headlines, but I don't know of any form of either that's more dangerous than the corruption and subversion of the democratic system itself—because when that's distorted the people don't have the full power to correct any other evils. That's why I do cartoons on some of these things that have been going on for years and that don't generally make big news. To people who know their way around in government the subjects may be old stuff; but until something is done about them they're still important.

I may be drawing pictures of characters with long white whiskers until I develop a complete set of my own.

10

Smoking in the Lobbies

WHEN I BEGAN DOING CARTOONS in Washington, I was considerably set up by the number of comments on them and the requests for the "originals." Whatever the cartoon, some reader, some representative, some organization felt that it was just dandy. I soon realized that this was not due to any magic in the drawing brush or to anything particularly bracing about the Washington climate. There are a lot of people and a lot of organizations in this city, and they represent a lot of viewpoints. There is nothing that's not of special interest to someone.

If I were to draw a cartoon about the starlings that crowd each other along the ledges of the Treasury Building, I'm sure there would be a call or a letter the next day from a Starlings Protective Society or a Starlings-Must-Go club. In this city, somebody always cares.

Back home I used to hear veteran reporter Bob Casey say with a sigh, whenever things got particularly fouled up, "It takes all kinds of people to make a world—and they're all here." It takes all kinds of interests to make a country, and they're all here in Washington, although they aren't always represented in proportion to their merits or to the numbers they speak for. There are good lobbies and bad ones, some with elaborate quarters, some with hole-in-the-wall offices—all working to win friends and influence people's representatives.

I do quite a few cartoons on the less public-spirited groups, but unfortunately their lobbyists don't make any effort to look like the characters I draw to represent them. They don't necessarily smoke big black cigars or develop large paunches; and they seldom wear vests on which the words SPECIAL INTERESTS OR LOBBIES are neatly lettered.

This makes it somewhat difficult to determine who are lobbyists and what are lobbies—as the government discovered after passing the Lobby Registration Act of 1946. *Congressional Quarterly,* that invaluable information service for newspapers, reported that representatives of about 2000 organizations had filed as lobbies between 1946 and 1951, with only about 300 regularly reporting expenses and sources of their incomes. The late Frank Buchanan, chairman of the 1950 Congressional committee investigating lobbying, estimated that there were at least three times as many pressure organizations as the number reporting to Congress. One Congressional-committee witness described the pressure groups as the "third chamber" of our national legislature. The lobbyists who comprise this "chamber" are many times the number of all the senators and representatives combined.

A lobby might be, among other things, a law office; a former legislator who exercises his privilege of returning to the floor of Congress to chat with his old colleagues; or a public information bureau—any of which might indignantly deny being in the pressure business. Buchanan called lobbying a billion-dollar industry, but wearily added that "the refrain from group after group was 'millions for education'—or public enlightenment—but not one cent for lobbying."

Ain't nobody here, boss, but jus' us educators.

This helpful educational work includes good old reading, writing, and 'rithmetic—reading and writing occasional speeches and bills for some congressmen; and making arithmetic easy to grasp in the form of campaign funds. This obviously doesn't go for most lobbies or most congressmen, but there's been enough of it to be worth a mention and a lot more looking-into.

We don't need to be concerned about pressure groups, according to one pleasant theory, because they tend to balance each other. That would be comforting if it were true. But too often the only balance that's achieved is the lightening of John Public's pockets on both sides at the same time. When

"I Didn't Quite Catch All The Names"

Oct 47

"What If I Should Meet Somebody I Know In There?"

Aug 49

the tax bills are framed, each of several interests demands concessions and exemptions to match those granted to others. This can give tax acts billion-dollar sets of loopholes that have all the artistic balance of a piece of Swiss cheese.

The oil lobby is one of the golden boys of the trade, and it nearly always has something on the fire—generally the consumer-taxpayer. When the "Boom

Boom Town

Feb 50

Town" cartoon was drawn, this lobby was drilling in more than one field. As one columnist pointed out, the oil lobby spends a great deal of money just to tell us that there is no oil lobby at all.

Another pressure group that raises its bulk in these drawings is the real-estate lobby, which is actually a collection of some of the most vocal leaders of organizations interested in housing—or the lack of it. This busy outfit, which was especially active after World War II, wore an injured air because of what it seemed to consider a conspiracy on the part of the American people to get adequate accommodations for themselves.

At the mere mention of building programs or rent controls, it has always been ready to let loose a flood of tears, letters, and pamphlets to show that the country is "overhoused." During the acute housing squeeze, one of its arguments—advanced against some of these cartoons—was that we were suffering not from too little housing but from "overconsumption of space." Presumably everything could have been solved by double-deck bunks and maybe storage cabinets for the kiddies. If there were such things as postwar medals this outfit surely should have received some for its valiant efforts, above and beyond the call of reasonable profits, to keep a rapidly growing population from getting itself lost in too many rooms.

A classic statement by one of its leaders, delivered in 1946, when an estimated million people were living "doubled-up," was that "we've got a gang in power [in Washington] who think solely in terms of the consumer, and usually

Aug 48

Jun 49

in terms of 'protecting' him." To the Democratic National Committee this little gem should have been worth its weight in building materials. But nobody could claim that there was political partisanship in a lobby that managed to bring upon itself rebukes from both President Truman and Senator Taft.

Time certainly flies, and almost before the postwar jam was over, we had a defense housing problem again. In a later chapter, there's a 1950 cartoon of

Room With A View

Apr 49

Speech On Housing

Mar 48

"Oops—Almost Forgot My Medicine Kit"

Dec 49

a couple of kids looking at a packing box which is "too small to play house." But in drawing that one I spoke too soon. By 1951 the stories of chicken-coop rentals in defense areas showed that nothing was too small to play house in, if the landlord was small enough to take advantage of the situation.

The real-estate lobby, which has considered Senator Taft to have a reddish tinge, at one time made an unsuccessful attempt to merge its efforts with those of the American Medical Association for a campaign against "socialized medicine" and "socialized housing," in which everybody could get together under one oxygen tent. The A.M.A., which declined the offer of co-operation, was doing pretty well for itself, thank you. Although new in the field, it managed to lead the entire list of registered lobbies in annual expenditures and talked in terms of million-dollar campaigns. The heads of this group originally organized a campaign against public health insurance—but they didn't stop there. They were like the surgeon who performed an operation before a medical audience and then proceeded to do a few more on the patient for encores.

The A.M.A., which had slapped a compulsory assessment on its members to fight compulsory health insurance, was so full of political vitamins and $25 assessment checks that it went into propaganda in a big way. Political diatribes by A.M.A. executives, made available to a waiting public in the outer offices of doctors, proved too much for some patients even in quarters where stomach pumps were available.

Some of this high-powered literature, evidently written under the impres-

"Watch That Blood Pressure, Doc"

Jan 52

"What's Going On? We Must Operate At Once"

Jun 50

sion that we were all about to take our tonsils to plumbers, pleaded with us not to spoil the doctor-patient relationship—which up to that time nobody had thought of spoiling. And while demanding that politics be kept out of medicine, the A.M.A. shoved medicine into politics up to the seventh cervical vertebra. I can be technical too, doctor; and if the medicos are going into political commentary in a big way, I might even take to scribbling a few Latin prescriptions into the cartoons.

The A.M.A. officially attacked the creation of a Public Welfare Department, which had been recommended by the Hoover Commission on Reorganization of the Government; and it also helped to kill bi-partisan proposals for aid to medical, dental, and nursing schools. The watch-that-blood-pressure cartoon was drawn after an A.M.A. official had refused to serve on the President's commission to survey the nation's health needs, and after the president of the A.M.A. had astonishingly asserted that there was no need for a survey at all. Individual doctors had expressed approval of some of the earlier cartoons, but this time one of the A.M.A.'s own local organizations asked for the drawing to hang in its headquarters to show its opinion of the national A.M.A. leadership.

In labeling general-membership organizations of this kind, I usually try to distinguish between the policy-making officials and the rank and file, who are not always in agreement with them. And I sometimes hear from individual members who say, "Thanks for labeling that cartoon character *Leadership* or *Spokesman*. Those fellows don't speak for all of us."

Big Parade

Jan 50

"Twist My Arm"

Jul 50

Some of the veterans' organizations throw a lot of weight around, but here again I've tried to avoid tagging an entire membership. The "professional vet" who works at being a veteran, wants coupons on his discharge certificate, and is \$100% more patriotic than anybody else, is obviously not the average vet who joins one of these organizations just for companionship, recreation, and public service.

"I Haven't Changed Anything Except The Crew"

Feb 51

"Hit Him Again—He's Still Breathing"

Jul 51

However much care is exercised in selecting the words in a cartoon, there is only room for a limited number of them. A complete summary of a piece of legislation and the arguments for or against it would tend to clutter up a picture. So if I do some cartoons about a general over-all pension scheme, after a while I'm sure to get a letter from a reader demanding to know what have I got against those poor disabled veterans who got themselves shot up for their country?

All I can do about that is to write back that I think disabled veterans are entitled to full benefits; but that the X.Y.Z. pension plan to provide solid-gold pogo sticks and lifetime annuities for 17,000,000 families of healthy veterans has nothing to do with those disabled in service.

I've already mentioned "farm politicians." With strong blocs in Congress, and both parties eager for the "farm vote," farm lobbies might not seem necessary. But they're active too, and they're not chicken-feed organizations. I think farmers are noble fellows entitled to reasonable protection, and I consume their products daily. But when Congress slips through a measure, as it did in 1951, drastically cutting imports of cheeses and other dairy products—while prices of domestic stuff soar to record heights—I think the rest of us are entitled to a little protection too.

A 1949 investigation of the potato-support program, made by John Ball of the Washington *Post,* revealed that in the state of Maine 31 individuals received U.S. government checks for more than $100,000 *each*—one of them for more than half a million dollars. It's just my guess, but I don't

Feb 51

Feb 52

"All He Wants Is Just That Little Switch"

Jun 51

Private Power Lines

Jul 49

think that those 31 fellows were "little farmers" who needed protection. I think there's a difference between dirt farming and gold digging, between a man with a hoe and a guy with a croupier's rake. And if it's all right with Congress, I'd like less of that kind of spring plowing in the U.S. Treasury.

Getting back to the "vested interests"—the utilities lobby is a high-voltage outfit, and like many others in this particular kind of "influence" business,

"How's That For Plugging The Loopholes?"

May 50

"He Never Knew What Hit Him"

Jul 51

"It's All Right—I've Got Him On A Leash"

Apr 47

"In Two Words, Yes And No"

Jun 49

it doesn't confine itself to the lobbies of Congress. It also goes to the country, warns of the danger of federal power and flood-control systems, and bleeds for "states rights." When the rivers overflow their banks, though, there's a mass swim for federal aid. But this is no fault of the utilities lobby, which does not personally create the floods. The utilities lobby, like the gas and oil lobby, disapproves of effective federal regulation, but when it's inevitable they like to be able to regulate the regulators.

Lobbying is a legitimate enterprise in a democracy, and the 1950 investigating committee didn't favor restricting it. But it recommended that lobbying activities be "carried on in a goldfish bowl," and said that the people had a right to know who was behind campaigns to influence Congress, directly or indirectly.

I couldn't agree more. But the goldfish bowl had better be a big one, and there's still the problem of getting some of the more slippery specimens into it.

11

The Nyever-Nyever Land

WITH SO MUCH to be improved upon in our own government, it's a pity that the Soviets, who keep telling us they've arrived at a state of political bliss, should keep the secrets of their perfection hidden behind an iron curtain. But reports on that Happy Land come through to us, along with former residents who have evidently found eternal joy a little monotonous. Of the many Elysian fields of Sovietland let us look first at the arts and sciences.

Musicians, writers, and artists in Soviet states do not have the usual disagreements with critics, and no one in that artistic heaven is left in doubt by mixed reviews. The criticism is official and final. It comes from sources that have arrived at complete, ultimate, undeviating truth. And when they say your stuff stinks, comrade, you'd better think so too.

The artists—especially those who feel that their hands might suffer from other work in colder climates—are properly grateful for the government's interest in their efforts and are quick to express their gratitude. In 1948, when the State took to the podium to sound a few warning notes to musicians, there was an immediate and responsive chorus of appreciation. So charming is the etiquette in these manners, and so well understood by all, that, when such composers as Prokofiev and Shostakovich thanked the government for its "fatherly concern" and "helpful chastisement," no one sounded the discordant cheer associated with the bourgeois Bronx—and hardly anybody threw up.

Later in 1948 Prokofiev evidently left the groove again, and the Soviet Musicians Union took the trouble to chide him for being "out of tune with the majority of Soviet music writers." Lucky Sergei to get such "helpful chastisement" twice in the same year! And small surprise that he had erred again, still trembling with joy as he must have been over the blessing of the earlier official recognition. It's a wonder he could get his hands on the piano at all.

Not having the Communist cauliflower ear for these things, I have never quite understood just what it is that makes some music "proletarian" as distinguished from that which displays "bourgeois formalism." In patriotic Soviet music perhaps the little half-notes thrust up their arms in clenched-fist salutes, while capitalistic notes just lie around the lower lines of the musical

Arrangement For Piano, Hammer And Sickle

"Say, I Think You've Got A Great Song Here"

Dec 48

Dec 49

staff with flags drooping, looking decadent. But the official critics can tell, unerringly—maybe even without looking or listening at all. When you have a real gift for these things, backed by the tuning instruments of the secret police, music is made easy.

Science, too, is simplified by official decisions. There everybody understands the basic rule that the Party line is the safest distance between two points; and everybody gets the points. For a time there was trouble in this scientific paradise when two schools of thought developed on the subject of eugenics. But the omniscient State stepped in with the final answer. The old Mendelian theory was out, and a new theory, developed by patriotic native Soviets, was in. No need to be concerned with blue eyes or brown eyes when you have the all-seeing eye of the State. No more the old fussing around with countless laboratory experiments in the slow, tedious process of trial and error: The Soviet scientist need worry only about one error followed by one trial.

In art, contrary to the opinion held by some of our native totalitarians who feel that "modern" painting is subversive, the Party line seems to be an extremely conventional one. As in the days of other emperors, there is a good deal of "court painting" and sculpture in which Stalin seems to come out somewhat bigger than life-size. The photographers manage to get the same effect in some of their pictures, which is only natural if they assume the proper kneeling position in such a Presence. I doubt whether they ask for "just one more" or direct the subject to wave or to "Smile, Mr. Premier." When a guy is sensitive about his height that way, he might not be in a good mood for joshing with cameramen, and who wants to shoot snow scenes all the time?

A New York art dealer once told me that a Soviet diplomat had been in to look over his current exhibit, and asked me if I could pick out the painting

"Thank You!" "Thank You!" "Thank You!"

May 49

the Russian had described as the only one of the bunch that "we would have." It turned out to be a painfully photographic little piece—appropriately enough, a still life. I should have guessed it. The bowl of fruit, depicted so realistically that you could almost pluck a pear from the canvas, would undoubtedly have a great proletarian appeal in a land where the proletariat does not always get to see these items in the round.

Soviet writers do not have the trouble that ours have, trying to put their thoughts into words. They don't really need to have any thoughts at all. In those Happy Lands where they have achieved a propaganda equality, everyone can have exactly the same thoughts as everyone else, everyone can say exactly the same things as everyone else. No unequal distribution in these commodities, even though there may be some slight disparities in unimportant items like living conditions.

But best of all the reader himself is saved from the dangers of liberalism, which so many worry about in our own country. Some of our super-patriots may well have a secret envy for a system where all ideas are subject to official review, where a ruling party does everything within its power to see that nothing unorthodox or "subversive" is spoken, printed, or even thought.

Politics, of course, is not subject to the confusion and debate that characterize our system. The Communist Party says it loves the people. And, ardent lover that it is, it anticipates their every wish. It knows what they want better than they know themselves. Every day is Christmas for a people who

"Now, Is Everything Perfectly Obscure?"

Oct 47

"We Now Bring You More Late Election Returns"

Mar 50

must always be thinking, of their ever-loving rulers: "Goodness! They've done things for us we'd never have thought of doing for ourselves."

Best of all, democracy itself has been made easy. The people of Happy Land know they have a democracy because their government tells them so. It thoughtfully saves them the tiresome thinking, the worrisome choosing and deciding that go with democracy in less enlightened countries. Have you ever stood in the voting booth, alone with your conscience, and wondered which were the best candidates, which policies the wisest? The voter in Happy Land does not find himself alone to face these problems. The Party is helpful; it gives him hot tips on which are the best candidates, and which—by a curious coincidence—are most likely to win. The voter has nothing to worry about except failing to mark his X in the right place. And even if this should happen the mistake is not beyond correction. The government can rub out the mistake—and the voter too.

Like the diplomats, but to a greater degree, Soviet athletes share the problems of competition with representatives of non-Communist countries. This problem is not so great in intra-mural events such as the 1951 soccer games between Soviet and East German teams. Here the Soviet team brought its own referees and scorekeepers—and, curiously enough, managed to win. The East Germans showed some disagreement by tearing up the field; but one should not expect proper etiquette from a people not yet fully indoctrinated with Soviet infallibility. It must be remembered that the East Germans showed a similar lack of understanding in the 1949 elections.

Post-Olympic Event

Aug 48

"Don't Worry About Nazis. Get Those Damn Liberals"

Feb 50

It is the international matches that provide the supreme test for Happyland athletes. In the 1948 Olympics, held in Britain, some of the stars from satellite states were so keyed up with the will to give their all for the Glorious Leader that they were unable to slow down to a trot even after the events were over. They continued on through the English countryside till they were lost to sight from their trainers, and never did get back to Paradise.

"It's The Same Thing Without Mechanical Problems"

Jan 49

The marvels of Soviet propaganda, unfettered by truth and free to soar like the dove of peace, are almost too well known to be recounted here. But I would like to dwell for a moment on a couple of its perennial themes. One of these is the incidence of crime in America. In cartoons and stories the Soviets are continually shocked by the shootings and gangsterism here.

Of course, we ourselves play up these items in our newspapers and movies more than most countries do—particularly more than countries which can't see their faults reflected and even exaggerated in a free press. But there must be more to it than that.

Crimes have always been committed in every land, under every type of government. What must really shock the Soviets is the ideological difference. Here we have shootings and other crimes. But these things are done on private initiative, in a loose, hit-or-miss fashion, and in defiance of the government. How much better are these things ordered in the Happy Lands! No "Murder, Incorporated" for them. Under the Soviets murder is a government monopoly, performed on a grand scale that makes our gangsterism piddling and amateurish. How shabby our crimes must seem, how inefficient our government which outlaws and prosecutes it, compared to the neat, well-ordered Soviet system under which people individually and by the thousands are dispatched in well-planned murders by the government itself. That's the real trouble with crime over here. It isn't neat enough and big enough. What can you expect from private enterprise?

It is the same with the irresponsible members of our press. There are some

The Gingerbread House

Apr 52

Observation Post

Oct 51

distortions here, but it is not consistent enough, and is not well enough organized. The press is not under the control of a government that makes lying and invective a fine art.

Our disputes between labor and management also figure in the Soviet handouts, and there are many people in our own country who share the view that these disagreements are tiresome and inconvenient. The Soviets have solved that one also. The government has a monopoly on labor as well as management. In the great proletarian government, all are potential laborers. And so versatile have the people become under this system, that millions who might never have thought themselves capable of performing hard physical labor have found themselves doing it. The State has made of hard labor not only an occupation but an adventure in which all can share.

How often we wish we could respond to the call of the great outdoors and get away from it all. In Sovietland the wish can be gratified. To the man lying awake at night, worrying about his family problems, the government can come like a Good Fairy waving its magic wand on his door. It can even come right through the door and wave its magic wand on the man himself. Then, in a twinkling, and before he's really aware *what's* happening he's whisked away—out of the dull daily routine, far from his petty problems, his office, his home—to exciting adventures in distant lands. Here, where the humdrum family life is left behind, he has the chance to cope with nature in the raw—and human nature at the same stimulating below-zero level. Mining! Lumbering! The rugged outdoor life that is the dream of every red-

"Always Glad To Loan My Neighbor A Shovel"

Feb 51

"You Got Any Special Rates For Natives?"

Dec 51

blooded man! The dream that makes every man-blooded Red tingle all over as the cold sweat stands out on his brow. And after the work is done, the long peaceful sleep. If he is a citizen of a satellite state, he might even get a chance for the supreme adventure of war itself. The Soviet State builds bodies. Mounds of them.

But the greatest Soviet triumph of all lies in the field of invention, particu-

"Set It Down Anywhere. We're Overcrowded Already!"

Feb 49

"To Give You An Idea How Effective It Is—
We're Beginning To Believe It Ourselves!"

Aug 50

"Oh-Oh, We May Need A New Building For
This One"

Nov 49

larly of history. Never before has one nation invented so many remarkable things and so much surprising history in so short a space of time. These are assembled behind the Kremlin walls in a massive building, adjoining the Propaganda Ministry. It is called the Smithsonovitch Institution. Figuring that the Soviets must be tired from all the inventing they've been doing for the last few years, I invented that one myself.

In this building are stored the first printing press with movable chains, the first atom, the first invisible robe woven for an emperor, the first reader, first base, first blush, and the first drink tonight. Here also is the first wheel, greatest invention of man, conceived by an ingenious Siberian who wanted a quicker way out. He unfortunately met with a fatal accident as he was passing a guard, but his invention lives on; and today behind the Kremlin walls hundreds of wheels are spinning madly in hundreds of heads.

It is only fitting that so many historic inventions and historical records should be kept from the idly curious, at least until the glue and the ink are dry. In a steel vault in the sub-basement of the Smithsonovitch is the first great propaganda piece—developed by a Russian, of course, and based on stories by Hans Christian Anderskof and the Brothers Grimmsky.

Admission is only to the faithful. Visiting hours 5 to 7. Quiet, please.

12

Fear and Smear

For the past few years the air of fear around here has been pretty thick. There's not always something you can put your finger on, but there are plenty of people anxious to put the finger on somebody.

Perhaps there is more nervousness in Washington than elsewhere because federal employees are sitting ducks these days. A government guy never knows when some anonymous witness might toss a fast accusation at him, and before he quite knows what's happened, he's liable to find himself out on the sidewalk and wearing a scarlet "D" for Disloyalty.

But I think the jitters have been pretty general, even though different people are twitchy about different things. With all our power and prosperity we rest as uneasily as the storybook princess who tossed and turned all night atop twenty eiderdown-stuffed mattresses because somebody had slipped a single pea beneath the bottom one.

What's been at the bottom of our insomnia has been a real concern about Communist agents. Unfortunately there *are* such things, and there have been real espionage cases. There are also atomic bombs and fast long-range bombers which can deliver a lot of bad things in small packages.

These things have made most of us feel less secure and have evidently thrown some of our old-time isolationists into a state of gibbering shock. But I don't think we need to go jumping out of windows or belting each other around in a general frenzy.

Close to 100 per cent of us in this country are against Communism. If you count unity by percentages on a thing like that, we ought to be about the most unified country in the world and we should be congratulating each other every day of the week. But we're not. We get to thinking about the damage that can be done by a small number of people and we look at each other out of the corners of our eyes.

There are two sides to the fear coinage now in circulation. One is the fear of what Communists might do to us; the other is fear of what fear itself is doing to us. As nice a summary of the present situation as I've seen appeared in the answers of a couple of girls to a question asked by an inquiring reporter in the Washington *Post's* "Reader Meter" column on June 11, 1952. The question was: "Do you think there is still validity in charges of Communism in the government?"

One girl said:

Well, I think there are, but I have no grounds to base it on. I would think that there are a lot more than we know about. And I think we should do something about it, too. People don't know how prevalent they really are. As I said, I have not real grounds for saying this. It's a belief of mine—you hear a lot about it and there must be something to it.

Another girl said:

I don't know if I should answer that. You see, I'm not a citizen—I'm English. I would imagine not—not that I know of. No, in England there isn't the same feeling of suspicion and insecurity. There are so few Communists, too, in this country. By the way, I'm not a Socialist either. There are so many wild charges going around in the United States. It makes me so mad—it reminds me of the technique Hitler used to breed dissension and suspicion among the people.

The same answers might be given to the whole question of Communist influence in the United States. A lot of people share the feelings of the girl who said frankly that she had no grounds on which to base her opinion but who thought we ought to "do something about it."

The trouble is—if you don't mind my peering over my spectacles and stroking my chin—that doing something, if it's the wrong thing, can be dangerous too. A panicky swimmer does a lot more thrashing around than a good one,

"You're With The State Department, I Presume"

Oct 47

"Okay, Honey—Put It On"

May 48

but he's just the guy to end up exhausted and engulfed by the very thing he fears.

Well, I think some honest people have been vaguely confused and panicky in just that way, endangering the freedoms and the security that we're trying to insure. That's why I've done cartoons like the one titled "Fire!"—which brought a letter from one reader exclaiming that nobody was hysterical, and

"Fire!"

Jun 49

"Hello—F.B.I.? My Neighbor Is Walking Around In The Un-American"

Jun 49

Political Pandora

Feb 50

demanding that I immediately turn myself in to the F.B.I. for having drawn such a cartoon. *Who's excited?*

Along the same line, the drawing of the woman at the telephone probably seems silly, but that's only because it was based on a news story that seemed silly. A woman who suspected her neighbor of being subversive had testified that the neighbor sometimes pulled down his blinds, sometimes had late parties, and sometimes went to the door to take in his morning paper without being fully clad.

Obviously a fellow like that is a suspicious character, and who knows but what he had propaganda tattooed between his toes ready to subvert the first chiropodist that came along. This is such stuff as dreams and accusations are made on. It is also an example of some of the miscellaneous unevaluated material in government files which some congressmen want turned over to them to spread on the public record.

I think we have reason to be concerned about Communism but no reason to scream and crawl under the carpet every time we catch sight of ourselves in a mirror.

It says somewhere that we fear the unknown. Few of us know much about advanced science, so this is well up on the list of things we're jittery about. Even when we had a monopoly on the atomic bomb, that didn't make us feel secure because it created new fears about what big secrets might get out. And within a couple of years after the first atomic blasts we already had the security shakes so bad that anyone who had missed out on recent history might have supposed we were the only country in the world that *didn't* have the bomb instead of being the only one that had it.

Some secrets did get out, and it only takes one or two espionage cases to create general talk about "all those fellows" giving away "all our secrets." But we don't get security by belaboring science in general, locking all the wrong doors, and shackling our own scientific progress.

Sep 49—On the news of the first Russian atomic explosion

"Never Mind About Breathing. This Is For Security"

Jun 49

"Let You In On A Secret. There's A Connection Here"

Sep 51

"Let's Face It—I'm Not A 100% American"

Jan 52

"Maybe We Can Get Together Sometime"

Feb 52

Many of the politicians who have been most fearful about our scientists don't seem to know a first-class secret from a book of first-year physics, and have just about enough scientific savvy to let the cold air out of a steam radiator. Or the cat out of the bag. As a matter of fact, some of the real national secrets that have leaked out have been disclosed by politicians themselves.

These secrets didn't exactly *leak* out. They were boomed out in statements and speeches. The cartoon of the sign hanging on the Capitol illustrates only one of many examples. A classic case was that of Senator Edwin Johnson's television broadcast of November 1, 1949. On this program, in which he expressed his fears about the ability of our scientists to keep their mouths shut, he revealed that we (which is to say our scientists) had made considerable progress in finding a way of detonating enemy bombs before they reached their targets, that we already had a super-bomb six times as effective as the first atomic bombs, and that we were working on another one (the hydrogen bomb) 1000 times more powerful than the Nagasaki bomb. This he cited as an example of the kind of secret that *must not* get out.

Great! Through the magic of radio and television, congressmen can impress everybody with what important secrets *they* know.

The Hickenlooper cartoon harks back to the time when this senator added his bit to the creation of national confusion by accusing the head of the Atomic Energy Commission of "incredible mismanagement." This charge, when investigated by a Senate committee, turned out to be simply a case of incredible hickenloopering. But the senator got some pretty high-power publicity out of it. There are some places where these fellows are not hipped on hush.

Most of our effective security work is done by our intelligence and counter-intelligence agencies, but this work is seldom seen. So there is a wide market for anti-Communist panaceas and "security" gadgets, many of which are

"How Do I Know You're A Good Security Risk?" *Jul 51*

"You Got Him Strung Up Yet, Boy?" *Jun 49*

about as effective as trying to catch rats by applying the third degree to everybody who likes cheese.

Some people put great store by non-disloyalty oaths, in which an employee is placed in the position of a suspected criminal and required to say, in effect, "Honest Injun, I'm not one of them." Since it is agreed that Communists have no compunctions about swearing falsely, these oaths can't very well serve to separate the sheep from the goats. The ineffectiveness of this kind of Mumbo-Jumbo does not, however, keep some of our fearful friends from demanding more and more of these negative oaths, insulting to more and more decent Americans. There are undoubtedly those who think we'd be a lot safer if our rubbish were carted away by garbagemen who had taken an oath.

There's no use going halfway with these things. If such methods are to be used, the system might as well be improved to require the person taking the oath to do so over a grave at midnight while sitting on a black cat. The oath could then be scratched on an old shingle and signed in blood. Not only would this added rigmarole insure absolute national security, but if the oath-taker held a toad in his left hand while raising his right hand aloft it would also eliminate warts.

A number of sincere people feel that in times like these we should toss overboard anybody about whose patriotism there is the slightest doubt. That sounds fine until we consider that the first thing that would be thrown overboard is the whole American idea of justice, under which people are innocent until proved guilty.

"You Mean Not Use The Ax At All?"

Aug 50

H-For-Hysteria Bomb

Mar 50

There is also the question: What kind of doubts in whose minds? In the past few years we've discovered that nobody's patriotism is above question by people who are fearful enough, or by people who are willing to capitalize on those fears.

In the fog of fear anyone might be hit and everyone looks suspicious. But in such fine weather for political murder and character assassination all the injuries haven't been accidental. Smear raised its ugly head and headlines.

When doubts, suspicions, and accusations are enough to do people in, then the fellows who beat their chests the loudest and do the most finger pointing become the most "patriotic," and you'd better shut up or they might point their fingers at you. When we try to get security that way, we end up with nobody being secure.

The national security then actually becomes a secondary matter while people knock each other down in frantic scrambles to salvage some security for themselves. Public and private officials become more intolerant, not out of fear for the country's safety but out of fear for their own safety—lest they be accused of not "doing something," of not being tough enough, not keeping pace with the trend. People become quicker to point the finger of suspicion at others because they are anxious to show that they are above suspicion themselves. And as Malvina Lindsay had a character in one of her columns express it, "It's getting so you're afraid to take cream in your coffee in a crowd that drinks it black."

When disagreement gets to be considered unpatriotic, then we have a whole country full of unpatriotic people. Some politicians have accused the Democratic administrations of the past twenty years of having been in cahoots with the Commies, and presumably all the people who voted for those administrations are guilty of unpatriotism-by-association. But that isn't all. Some of those same politicians consider large sections of the Republican party, particularly the Eastern and Western branches of it, to be unpatriotic too—and presumably the people who voted for such Republicans are also guilty of unpatriotism-by-association. In the end everybody is unpatriotic except thee and me—and sometimes I think even thee are unpatriotic.

The principle of guilt by association, accusation, and assassination has a familiar ring. It's the same "security" system used by Those Fellows in Russia who are always conducting purges and apparently always finding it necessary to conduct still more purges. Under that system it's dangerous to hang up a picture of anybody except the Number One Man, because anyone else might suddenly be purged—and there you'd be with the purgee's picture hanging on your wall, and maybe yourself hanging right next to it.

All this is also a little reminiscent of the French Revolution in which a leader of the revolution one month might find himself in the tumbrel the following month because he hadn't made enough heads roll.

Well, I think what's been going on in this country has been a kind of unorganized Un-American Revolution, in which the smear-bucket brigade has been trying to sack our institutions while hollering at us to look farther and farther under the bed for subversives.

The Fear-and-Smear racketeers have hijacked a legitimate public concern about Communism and steered it down their own dark alleys.

They run around with smudgepots, crying, "Where there is so much smoke there must be fire!" They demand that more and more heads roll, that more and more reputations be strung up. Administrators, judges, and even members of the United States Supreme Court are accused of being "soft on subversives" for following traditional American standards of justice.

By May 2, 1952, President Truman had become alarmed about the course of his own federal loyalty program. He said:

> We have a right to protest against the creation of an atmosphere in which a charge is a conviction in the public mind despite the lack of evidence. . . . The loyalty program was designed to protect innocent employees as well as the government. When I set it up, I intended it to expose the guilty and at the same time to safeguard the rights and reputations of those who were innocent. But I have become increasingly concerned in recent months by attempts to use the loyalty program as a club with which to beat government employees over the head. Political gangsters are attempting to pervert the program into an instrument of intimidation and blackmail, to coerce or destroy any who

Loyalty Test — **"Don't Mind Me—Keep Right On Working"**

Jul 47 — *Jul 47*

dare oppose them. These men and those who abet them have besmirched the reputations of decent, loyal public servants. They have not hesitated to lie, under cover of Congressional immunity, of course, and repeat the lies again and again. . . . These tactics contain the seeds of tyranny. Can we be sure that people who employ such tactics are really loyal to our form of government, with its Bill of Rights, its tradition of individual liberty? The fact is that they are breaking these things down. They are undermining the foundation stones of our Constitution. I believe such men betray our country and all it stands for. I believe they are as grave a menace as the Communists; in fact, I think they're worse than Communists and I think they're partners with them.

If we could get more and more security by eliminating more and more people, regardless of actual evidence, then the maximum security should be achieved by firing *all* government employees, leaving only a few deaf-and-dumb janitors to sweep up what's left of the government. To avoid the possibility of a soldier pointing a gun the wrong way, we might also disband the Army. And on the principle that dead men tell no tales, we could liquidate all scientists and engineers. There would then be nobody to give away any secrets—and, in fact, no more secrets to be given away.

This way, as the saying goes, lies madness.

But there is method to the madness of the Fear Dealers who are trying to remake our country in their own image. They scream "Communism" or "Un-Americanism" whenever they want an excuse for knifing somebody or something they don't like. They bellow that they're protecting us from subversion while at the same time actually subverting just about everything this country

Wrong Number — *Jan 50*

"Hello, Dear, And All You Boys On The Wire Taps" — *Jan 50*

stands for. And they have tried to take over the word "Americanism" in exactly the same way that their Communist counterparts have tried to take over "Peace" and "Democracy."

In this through-the-looking-glass era, beliefs in the most basic American principles are coming to be regarded as unpatriotic. Communists are always talking about equality, freedom, and the Bill of Rights—and you don't want

"We Now Have New And Important Evidence"

May 50

people to think you're a Communist, do you, pal? And about this business of speaking up when others are attacked—you've heard of guilt-by-association, haven't you, pal?

Occasionally I read an editorial comment which says with phony philosophy something like this:

> We hear some people say there isn't the freedom to speak that there used to be; but as long as anybody can still complain we don't reckon there's anything to complain about. Last time we looked out the window the little ole world was still revolvin' around on its axis, and in a little ole world that keeps on adoin' that, we figure everything is bound to be pretty much all right.

To this kind of thing I always feel like saying: By jingo, I reckon everything *will* come out all right, at that—and no thanks to you, fatmouth.

When we come out all right after attacks on freedom, it's because there were people who got in there and slugged back. At the time the crates-of-books cartoon was drawn, the Committee on Un-American Activities had written many colleges to send it copies of the textbooks they were using. There were so many howls of protest against this obvious attempt at censorship of education that the committee hastily backed down, mumbling something about having had nothing in mind at all—just wanted to see the books. It must have found all those books and all those protests very educational, particularly the latter.

There are constant demands that schoolbooks should be subject to review

World Powers No. 1 And 2 — *Aug 49*

"Okay—Now To Find Somebody That Can Read" — *Jun 49*

by self-appointed censors with no particular qualifications beyond ownership of pencils, scissors, and red-white-and-blue hatchets. But the most ambitious attempt at literary review came in the spring of 1952, when a U.S. congressman proposed that all the books in the Library of Congress should be screened to purge that institution of "subversive" reading matter. This vigilant soul evidently wanted to make sure that none of his colleagues would be led astray in case any of them should some time walk into that hotbed of public informa-

"You Read Books, Eh?"

Apr 49

tion unaware. Other advocates of censorship, struck by the sweep and scope of this idea, could only ask themselves, Why didn't *we* think of that?

Some states, cities, and semi-public organizations have their own Un-American committees—Witch-Hunters Junior Grade—but filled with no less zeal than their Big Brothers. The little Un-American committees, official and unofficial, are great on compiling lists of people they want to get rid of. This is a big advance over the old method of hexing people by sticking pins into little images of them. A list is easier and far more effective. As a matter of fact, it's a prime requisite in the Un-American racket. Every Gilbert and Sullivan fan knows that a list is an essential prop for a Lord High Executioner, which is what each of these groups sets itself up to be.

The Committee on Un-American Activities boasts an unchecked list of over a million names, but this needn't make anyone feel that he's too small to go into the business himself. In this occupation, there's no such thing as being too small. You can start with practically no list at all, and through the magic of guilt-by-association you can make it grow like mushrooms in a dank cellar. The other committees in the racket are always glad to spread the bad word, and they'll even tear off a sprig of names from their own lists to give you a start. All you have to do is supply your own fertilizer.

Practically anything will do for a beginning—a bit of gossip, an old letterhead, or just a personal animosity toward somebody. With any of these things

"Wheeee!"

Jun 49

"And Keep An Eye On A Cake My Wife Has In The Oven"

Mar 50

and a title that sounds patriotic, you begin to fan out on the chain-letter or pyramid-club principle. You add the names of other people who know these people, or who belong to the same organizations as those on your starting list—or who just think some of the same things as these people. A million names can be lined up with no trouble except for the bookkeeping work; but the amateur should be warned that there is a danger in letting the list get *too* big.

For example, if you get hold of a good letterhead of some wartime relief organization, you find the name of somebody on it who might be, say, a fellow traveler. This makes the letterhead an important collector's item, a real find. An overzealous amateur might quickly add to his list all the people on the letterhead, including names like Herbert Hoover and Winston Churchill. These tend to spoil the effect.

Goodness knows you don't have to be very selective in the Un-American business, but you have to be a little careful or else *everybody* will laugh at you. An old hand like Senator McCarthy understands these fine points—and one Senate committee had to press him pretty hard for distinguished names he had overlooked on *his* collection of letterheads. When the compilers of *Red Channels* got up their blacklist they didn't include the names of people like Mrs. Roosevelt. You have to be a little smart about those things. I didn't say *very*.

What's really impressive is the way the Un-American lists support each other. It's all very fraternal, and plagiarism is actually invited. This makes it possible to say that a victim is on the list of the Committee on Un-American Activities, the Tenney Committee of California, for example, the Dry Gulch Super-Duper Patriotic Committee, and the Red Hot White and Blue Committee of Lower Sixteenth Street. That is what passes in the trade for corroborative evidence.

I think we ought to award the badge of Un-Americanism to some of those who have tried so hard to pin it on others.

They've earned it, and it's time we let 'em have it.

13

The Screaming Whimwhams

EVERY SO OFTEN a question is raised as to how much editorial attention should be given to undesirable characters who seem to thrive on publicity. The editorial-page notice such a person receives often depends on how much he's been able to get himself into the public eye, but this is only a rule of sore thumb. Sometimes the issue raised by the character is worth attention even if he is not.

Senator McCarthy got himself in the public eye like a sack of soot, and there was not much doubt about his figuring in cartoons and editorials. He often refers to himself in the third person as if admiring himself from afar or afraid that the name might escape somebody. Whether or not he was gratified by the popular use of the word "McCarthyism" I don't know. In any case, that word seems to have originated in the elephant-and-smear-buckets cartoon, which was first published in March 1950. There's nothing particularly ingenious about the term, which is simply used to represent a national affliction that can hardly be described in any other way. And if anyone else has a prior claim on it, he's welcome to the word and to the junior senator from Wisconsin along with it. I will also throw in a set of free dishes and a case of soap.

The various interesting activities of this senator cannot be compressed into a few pages, but continuing this condensed saga of Fear-and-Smear, we can look back for a moment to the time when he achieved his peculiar fame.

By February 9, 1950, the air was so charged with fear that it took only a very small spark to ignite it. That very small spark was Joseph R. McCarthy, who delivered what was evidently scheduled to be a routine political attack and found that he had the country by the ears.

He said, "I have here in my hand a list of 205 that were known to the Secretary of State as being members of the Communist Party and who nevertheless are still working and shaping policy in the State Department." This is the old list-trick with sleight-of-hand added. With this refinement you don't even need to bother with the minor work described in the preceding chapter: you can just palm an old laundry list. Come to think of it, that may be what McCarthy held in his hand. But judging from the later fluctuations in his numbers, it's more likely that he was absent-mindedly going over some stock quotations.

In more normal times he might have been greeted by some such old-fashioned American expression as "put up or shut up." Even a modest curiosity might have prompted his listeners to ask for some evidence. But they asked nothing except that he scare the pants off them.

"You Mean I'm Supposed To Stand On That?"

Mar 50

Joe was certainly ready to oblige—although, heady with all that power, he seemed to have some trouble focusing on that list in his hand. A few days later he said, "I have in my hand 57 cases of individuals who would seem to be card-carrying members or certainly loyal to the Communist Party . . ." Fifty-seven is an interesting number, and at this time he was possibly holding in his hand a Heinz soup-can label. His listeners had already been thrown for a loss of 148 names, but they came back for more.

His next unlucky number was 81, and he then backed down to "one top espionage agent." It was the greatest drop since the crash of October 1929, but the McCarthy supporters were still bullish—as were the McCarthy speeches. I did a cartoon of a sweating McCarthy in the spotlight saying "My next number will be—"; and following the collapse of his "one top espionage agent" case on which he was going to stand or fall, I drew a cartoon showing him falling flat on his face.

McCarthy has shown an amazing agility in leaping from one charge to another, ducking into his Congressional immunity when smearing individuals, and ducking out on replies by his victims.

"I hold in my hand," to borrow a phrase, the transcript of a radio broadcast, "Reporters' Roundup," for September 13, 1951. William H. Lawrence of the New York *Times* was speaking:

LAWRENCE: Senator McCarthy, this whole issue started back with your Wheeling, West Virginia, speech when you said there were either 57 or 81 or 205 card-carrying Communists in the State Department. Now my first question is—what evidence have you offered of any card-carrying Communists in the State Department?

MCCARTHY: One has been convicted and sentenced to five years.

LAWRENCE: What one was that, sir?

MCCARTHY: William Remington.

LAWRENCE: As I understand it, Senator, Mr. Remington was employed by the Commerce Department, not by the State Department. Let's be precise, now, what have you offered in evidence as to people in the State Department?

MCCARTHY: Just a minute, Mr. Lawrence. Mr. Remington was technically on the Commerce Department's payroll, but he was working *with* the State Department—and besides a Communist is just as dangerous in the Commerce Department as in the State Department. And I intend to dig them out whether they're in Commerce or State . . .

Mr. Lawrence then pointed out that Remington not only wasn't a State Department employee, but that his name had been brought up long before McCarthy made his original speech.

This interesting exchange does not represent McCarthy in his more imaginative moments, but it's as good as any for students of his technique. He does not answer the question, but he is against *all* Communists in *all* departments—which of course, we all are—and off he goes in another cloud of smoke.

Just to keep the record straight, McCarthy—despite his keen interest in finance—never accepted former Senator Millard Tydings' offer to give him $10,000 (later raised to $25,000) if he would prove to a U.S. grand jury his charges about "State Department Communists"—card-carrying or plain.

One more example of the McCarthy technique. This one is on me.

In 1950 the State Department began distributing abroad a booklet of my

"Joe—Yoo Hoo—Joe"

Apr 50

cartoons against Communism. At this writing about a million copies of that booklet have been published in a dozen or so languages, nearly all editions printed in foreign countries.

The original printing was an English-language edition which the Washington *Post* helped prepare and for which I gave the reprint rights and supplied a foreword. These booklets were ordered for the State Department by the Washington *Post* from a Silver Spring (Maryland) lithographic company. The State Department paid the printing cost of its 50,000 copies, and the Washington *Post* gave the department half of the 20,000 additional copies which the *Post* had bought for itself. No copyright fee, no royalties, no charge for compiling the booklet, no profit for the *Post*, and of course not a penny for me. Records of such expenditures are easily available.

Now step closer, observe carefully, and watch the sleight-of-hand. This is the way it comes out in a booklet by McCarthy:

> After weeks of work these men [Congressman Hill of Colorado and a newspaperman named Willard Edwards] uncovered a large number of secret contracts made by the State Department, which showed that the department used a $27,000,000 slush fund in 1950 to subsidize a number of radio commentators, cartoonists, writers and publishers. For example, the State Department paid over $2,000 for a book of Herbert Block's cartoons entitled *Herblock Looks At Communism.*

In the McCarthy version the contracts are "secret," they are "uncovered," and the State Department funds are a "slush fund" used to "subsidize" people. But McCarthy apparently knows better. When he had earlier put out this

CONGRESSIONAL IMMUNITY
VICTIMS OF McCARTHY ACCUSATIONS
HERBLOCK
"I HAVE THE NAMES OF 57* COMMUNISTS IN THE STATE DEPARTMENT"
"I SHALL BE WILLING AND EAGER TO GO BEFORE ANY COMMITTEE AND GIVE THE NAMES AND ALL THE INFORMATION AVAILABLE"
"ON THE DAY WHEN I SAY ANYTHING ON THE SENATE FLOOR WHICH I WILL NOT BE WILLING TO SAY OFF THE FLOOR I WILL RESIGN FROM THE U.S. SENATE"
McCARTHY
HERBLOCK

"Step Outside And Say That" — Mar 50

"Stop Ganging Up On Me!" — Apr 50

story orally, Murrey Marder, a Washington *Post* reporter who was present, asked him, "Do you mean that Herblock received any money from the State Department?" To which McCarthy quickly replied, "I didn't say that."

In repeating the story in his booklet, McCarthy, of course, didn't say *that*.

Just incidentally, the Washington *Post* is an independent newspaper which in 1951 editorially called for the resignation of Secretary of State Dean Acheson. And the State Department is still reprinting and distributing abroad my cartoons against Communism.

The Margaret Chase Smith cartoon was drawn after the declaration of conscience issued by Mrs. Smith and six other Republican senators who were *not* urging Joe—as Senator Taft was—to "keep talking, and if one case doesn't work out, proceed with another."

What gave rise to the boy-and-the-fence cartoon was the fact that McCarthy had demanded and received radio time to reply to a speech by President Truman which referred to smear attacks but did not mention McCarthy by name. The senator did not, however, demand time or space to reply to a similar statement by the Roman Catholic bishops of the United States who declared, in November 1951, that "dishonesty, slander, detraction and defamation of character are as truly transgressions of God's commandments when resorted to by men in political life as they are for all other men."

Well, a fellow can't answer *all* the statements that don't mention him by name.

"Go Upstairs And Wash Your Hands"

Jun 50

"Stop That! McCarthy Will Demand Space For A Reply"

Aug 51

"Help! I'm Being Followed"

Oct 51

"Now, You Said You Wanted To Be Heard?"

Feb 52

It would hardly be proper to devote this much space to McCarthy without some mention of the man who is the object of his admiration on the other side of the political aisle. That is Senator Pat McCarran. This senator is less flamboyant than McCarthy, as befits his role in the act, which is that of a "judge" before whom McCarthy is willing to lay his "facts." Since some of McCarthy's "facts" seem to come from the McCarran Committee, this makes a nice, cozy, vicious circle.

As head of the Senate Judiciary Subcommittee on Internal Security, McCarran acts with a great air of judiciousness, thoughtfully giving the widest possible scope to those whose opinions he wants spread on the record—and thoughtfully giving somewhat less scope and more intensive grilling to those who disagree or who have been denounced before his committee. When hearing favored witnesses, the McCarran Committee has expansively ruled that hearsay evidence is perfectly admissible before it. But it does not wish to listen to prepared statements, given under oath, by victims of such hearsay.

Pat McCarran as head of the Senate Judiciary Committee has a high regard for Pat McCarran, head of the Senate Judiciary Subcommittee on Internal Security—and complete faith in the latter's ability to decide all security matters. In his capacity as Grand Pooh-bah of Security, he managed to block confirmation of the Nimitz Commission, which the President had appointed to examine our laws and procedures on internal security. Here are the names

"Can't Take Any Chance On Having Varmints Around"

Sep 50

All Quiet Along The Potomac

Jun 51

of the members of that commission which McCarran stopped before it ever got started:

Fleet Admiral Chester W. Nimitz, chairman;

Miss Anna Lord Strauss, president of the National League of Women Voters, vice-chairman;

The Right Reverend Karl Morgan Block, Bishop of the Episcopal Diocese of California;

Former United States Senator (Republican) John A. Danaher of Connecticut;

Harvey S. Firestone, Jr., chairman of the Firestone Tire and Rubber Company;

Charles H. Silver, vice-president of the American Woolen Company of New York;

The Most Reverend Emmet J. Walsh, Coadjutor Bishop of the Catholic Diocese of Youngstown, Ohio;

Russell C. Leffingwell, director of J. P. Morgan & Company and former Assistant Secretary of the Treasury;

William E. Leahy, Washington attorney.

McCarran was now in the position of the cannibalistic sailor in W. S. Gilbert's poem, who said:

Oh, I am a cook and a captain bold
And the mate of the *Nancy* brig
And a bo'sun tight, and midshipmite,
And the crew of the captain's gig.

After disposing of the Nimitz Commission, he was the Fleet Admiral too, and chief petty officer in charge of security.

But in all his many capacities he is the tireless investigator and prosecutor of Un-McCarran Activities. On one occasion he summoned to his office officials of the State Department, who were astonished to find awaiting their arrival the representative of the government of McCarran's friend Franco. The senator then demanded that the U.S. government officials explain to the Spaniard why Franco was not receiving more aid.

"Always Happy To Take The Word Of A Lady"

Sep 51

"There Ain't A Good 100% Spaniard In The Lot"

"Well, If It Doesn't Work Right Why Don't You Put Your Thumb On The Scale?"

Jul 51 *Oct 50*

A fellow like that is obviously just the boy to decide what's good Americanism in this country—and who can blame him for not wanting people like Admiral Nimitz poking around in the work that he and McCarthy have laid out for themselves?

McCarthy and McCarran gave a big boost to the Fear-and-Smear business which had already reached dizzying heights and now got even dizzier. Anyone could get into the act. Little groups of telephone and writing-desk vigilantes, determined to purge the entertainment field of people they didn't like, found that they could get into other people's acts too. Some of the radio executives and sponsors showed an eagerness to please that matched the high-power heartiness of their commercials.

You could reach NOW for your favorite blacklist, write a dozen letters of fifty words, more or less, and tear off the head of anybody on the program. No fuss, no bother, no embarrassing questions, and no after-rinse. Just a few words about what entertainer you're suspicious of, drop it into the mailbox—yes, any mailbox—and zip, zip, off comes the head, slick as a whistle, ready to be mounted and hung over your mantel, courtesy of this station and the Itsy Bitsy Folding Backbone Company.

Some of the program directors took to having their actors "cleared" with list-makers to save listeners the bother of even writing a few letters.

The comparison between these purges and the Soviet policing of the arts is worth a passing thought. Like the Russian government, which can tell a non-proletarian musical note when it hears one, our vigilantes evidently have a keen ear for the subversive tone of voice. I've never heard anything on the radio waves that sounded dangerous in a way that a good seasick remedy couldn't cure. And I don't know how you'd overthrow a government by the lilt with which you sing "Toot Toot Tootsie," or the inflection you give to the lines of the soaporific operas.

Perhaps it has something to do with vibrations, and if you say "No, John, No" often enough, with just the right timbre in your voice, Radio City and the Capitol in Washington might come crashing down like the walls of Jericho. There seem to be people who do a lot of thinking about these possibilities. Well, they do a lot of worrying and letter-writing anyhow.

This great government is not going to fall for any lack of effort on their part to wreck careers in the entertainment field. There should be a medal for such heroic conduct above the call of duty and behind the back of the hand—possibly a design of a couple of palms around an open larynx, or maybe just a simple cluster of poison oak.

The cartoon "I Don't Need You to Protect Me, Junior" appeared after a couple of outbreaks of physical violence, including one in which a man was beaten up by fellow plant workers, apparently for having signed a phony peace petition. This drawing got a big favorable response, because a lot of people were jolted by the stories of bodily assaults. But it would be hard to decide which form of vigilantism should win the lead-lined boxing gloves. In some ways the poison pen is mightier than the club.

"I Don't Need You To Protect Me, Junior"

Jul 50

"... Adder's Fork, And Blind-Worm's Sting, Lizard's Leg, And Howlet's Wing ..."

Jun 49

"Down In Front!"

Sep 50

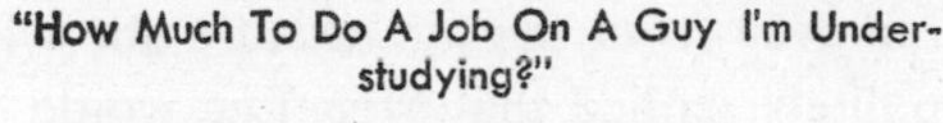
"How Much To Do A Job On A Guy I'm Understudying?"

Sep 50

The husband of one entertainer who was smeared off the air gave a talk to an association of radio artists, in which he pointed out some of the things they would have to expect if they became victims of similar attacks. Among other things to get accustomed to was the matter of being wakened in the middle of the night by anonymous, threatening phone calls. And then there were incidental expenses and inconveniences like having to get someone to accompany your children to and from school.

Such wonderful results from just a few calls and letters! Such remarkable multiple-action from copying a few names off a list in this new, easier-than-ever way! It was enough to make the Fear-and-Smear boys come out from under their rocks and dance in the alleys.

What really gave me a cold chill, though, was a conversation with a visiting publisher after the "Down in Front" and the "Understudy" cartoons appeared. He was somewhat troubled as we discussed the general problem, and then said, "But, Herb—you don't *know* that these people are innocent." This, coming from a newspaperman who might reasonably be concerned about the threat to freedom of communications, struck me as a startling illustration of how far we had already come from the basic idea that people are innocent until proved guilty.

One radio official who remembered that old American principle was Robert E. Kintner, president of the American Broadcasting Company. When an Illinois official of the American Legion demanded that Gypsy Rose Lee be removed from the air because she was listed in *Red Channels,* Mr. Kintner politely replied that Miss Lee would not be removed till there was evidence to warrant such action. No evidence was ever presented.

Mr. Kintner received radio's Peabody Award for his stand, and I think he deserved it. But I think also that it's an awful reflection on the radio industry that so simple and obvious an act of decency and American fair play should

"Say, What Ever Happened To 'Freedom-From-Fear'?"

Aug 51

have been one of its most outstanding acts of public service.

The press has its own responsibilities and problems with Fear-and-Smear. In an address at the University of Colorado, Alan Barth, author of *The Loyalty of Free Men,* pointed out that newspapers have allowed themselves to be used by unscrupulous politicians as instruments of "punishment by publicity." He said:

> When we publish in headlines that Senator McCarthy has spewed out wild charges of treason or espionage against a career foreign service officer or an economic adviser to the President or a university professor having no connection whatever with the government, we do the Senator's dirty work for him and we inflict on his victim an irreparable injury.

Commentator Elmer Davis and Editors Erwin Canham of the *Christian Science Monitor* and Gideon Seymour of the Minneapolis *Star and Tribune* are among others who have also spoken publicly about the current problem of how to print the truth without helping to spread lies.

Everything in a newspaper involves selection and helps to form impressions in the readers' minds. And I sometimes think that the "opinion" influence of editorial writers, columnists, and cartoonists is small compared to the generally unintentional editorial influence of the men in the news department.

If a respectable Senator Jones, minding his own business and waiting for a taxi, is kicked in the stomach by a drunken Senator Blank, it seems to me less than fair to say:

JONES AND BLANK IN STREET BRAWL

With smear stories the damage is greater. Denials seldom catch up with accusations and usually serve only to tighten the tie-up of the victim's name with the charge made against him.

It can't be much satisfaction for an innocent man to read a follow-up story, even if it's given equal space and prominence, that says:

JONES DENIES HE'S A COMMUNIST

or

JONES DENIES HE'S A CROOK

As you turned to this page, these headlines jumped out at you. You could scarcely escape the impression that this Jones fellow was certainly mixed up in some bad business. This is the impression that sticks with many readers—or headline-glancers—even in stories of denials, in which the victim is getting his best break. As one newspaperman recently observed, *denies* has become one of the dirtiest words in the language.

What's to be done about all this isn't exactly in my department, but it's of interest to a lot of us on the sidelines of the news as well as to the editors, reporters, and headline-writers who have to grapple with hot copy.

We might follow up attempted character assassinations just as we do the more physical types of violence. If a body is found with a knife in the back we want to know who was at the other end of that blade; and if it was cold-blooded murder we want to make sure that the criminal is out something more than just the loss of the knife. Well, a person can be stabbed by a statement these days. It's possible to get "lead poisoning" from a slug of type as well as from a bullet.

When Anna Rosenberg was up for confirmation as Assistant Secretary of Defense, an attempt was made to brand her as a Communist. At about the same time, Secretary of the Interior Oscar Chapman also became the victim of a smear attack. In both cases the charges turned out to be completely groundless. But there was no penalty for the character assassins in law and there was little in "punishment by publicity" to discourage other attempts of the same kind. Political policies of newspapers and of public figures involved in stories like these have nothing to do with such cases. Fair is fair and news is news. Who did what to whom and why?

In June 1952, when the State Department alerted its customs agents to be on guard against an attempt by Owen Lattimore to depart for an iron-curtain country, this was big news, but it was not all of the story. Lattimore, who

"Now, One Thing More To Investigate—"

Another Racket To Crack Down On

Dec 50

Dec 50

knew nothing about the action until it became public, declared that he hadn't even considered such a trip, but the State Department insisted that its information came from "official sources" and that it knew what it was doing.

Reporter Alfred Friendly of the Washington *Post* was not satisfied to let it go at that. He dug out and published the fact that the State Department had acted on a tip which was completely phony. Within a week after Friendly's story appeared, the tipster was indicted by a federal grand jury in Seattle, and the State Department made a public apology. Readers across the country got the answer to the question "True or false?" They also found out whodunit. Phony tipsters found out that there can be a penalty for giving false information to government agents. Public officials discovered that there are dangers in embracing the methods of McCarthyism.

Newspapers can also alert their readers with background material. When a McCarthy keeps trotting out various versions of the same old story, we can let our readers in on this. There's no use acting as if he's presenting a red-hot dish when he's actually serving up a tossed salad of leaves from the same wilted list he's been clutching in his hand for a couple of years.

A United States senator actually enjoys a double immunity. First, he can slander a citizen on the floor of Congress without fear of legal reprisal; and second, he is protected from the same kind of attack upon himself because it is literally against the rules for one congressman to reflect upon the integrity of another. The newspapers have a kind of second-hand immunity in dealing with Congressional stories, because they are legally privileged to publish charges made in Congress or before Congressional committees which would be libelous if they came from any other source.

Responsible newspapers don't want their printing ink used to load the spray guns of smear artists. They don't want to be Charley McCarthys for the voice of a Joe McCarthy. And they don't want to maim honest reputations in print any more than they would want their trucks to run down citizens in the streets if they were also privileged to do *that* in delivering the news about Congress. But they have an obligation to print the news. And there, as the fellow says in the play, is the rub.

Hot news has become a hot problem.

14
Shop Talk

I THINK IT WAS FANNY BRICE who used to do a skit in which she asked a group of people, "Have you ever heard the story of Hiawatha?" Her listeners immediately chorused, "Yes!" Whereupon she said, "Then listen, and I will tell you. . . ."

Well, I just happen to have here in my pocket a few notes I've jotted down in answer to questions about the cartoon business, and now that you haven't asked, here they are.

One of the most frequent inquiries is, "How far in advance do you work?" The answer is: Just from one day to the next. And this is immediately followed by the surprised question, "Why don't you get ahead?" I hear this all the time, and it makes me feel like a wastrel—just living from hand to drawing paper, never giving a thought to the morrow, never putting anything away for a nice sunshiny day. The bees and the ants and the squirrels are storing up all manner of goodies, and here I am without two bright new drawings to rub together. That's just as well because when you rub them together they smear. But the point is I haven't got anything laid aside.

One reason is that in doing cartoons about current events you can't get very far ahead unless you are also something of a crystal gazer, which I'm not. I envy the comic-strip men, who can control the actions and plan the futures of the characters they draw. At least I envy them until I think of the effort that must be required to do the four panels a day and half-pages for Sunday that most of them turn out. Then I wonder how *they* ever get ahead.

One picture seems to be a day's work for me. And for some perverse reason, on the days when I want to get through early to catch a train I always seem to think of ideas for drawings like the one of the airplanes here—or something that involves intricate mechanical devices—or picturing sixty people riding horses in different directions. This may be due to coincidence or to conscience, but I've missed a lot of trains that way.

Oddly enough, extremely simple cartoons can be troublesome too. Take for example a real "nothing picture" like the "White Paper" cartoon of the blank page edged in black. After that one appeared, there was a stream of laughing inquiries about whether I was out of town long, did I enjoy my game

"We'll Have To Do Something About This Some Day"

Nov 49

White Paper On The Peron Dictatorship

Mar 51

of golf that day, and—just to settle a bet—did it take five minutes to do or did I dawdle around and stretch it out to ten? Let me tell you about that one. This isn't particularly interesting but it's awfully exclusive, because up to now every time I've started to tell about that day's work everybody got to laughing so hard at the word "work" that I couldn't get any further.

In this reduced size you probably can't make out any of the type in that cartoon except the name of the newspaper. You'll just have to take my word that there is an "ear" in the upper right-hand corner which translates to "Edition of 0 pages," and beneath the title a line of type which includes the date, and the rest of the things that customarily go on that line.

Since there were no copies of *La Prensa* available at the time, I had to go across town, beg an old copy from the Library of Congress, have the title photostated, and then have the rest of the type duplicated—after first getting a Spanish translation of the current date, volume number, etc. This was followed by an all-thumbs job of pasting these odds and ends of printers' proofs into place. The whole thing took longer than an ordinary cartoon.

This may seem like a lot of wasted energy, but the cartoon was timed for the opening of a conference of Pan-American foreign ministers in Washington, and the Latin diplomats were all familiar with the famous Argentine newspaper. It turned out that the details of this cartoon edition of *La Prensa* hadn't gone unnoticed, and I felt it was worth the trouble. I'm not sure, though, that it was worth the kidding I got for the next couple of weeks about having let myself off easy on that one.

Foreign-language phrases have always been something of a problem for this student, who never got beyond a few textbook lines about putting le book on le boy who is under la table. The De Gaulle cartoon ran when a French election came along just as the MacArthur theme song was going strong. The title on it is simple enough, but you'd be surprised at the difference of opinion there was around the office about the proper translation of "old soldiers" in this context. I finally phoned the French embassy and asked a press attaché how to say "old soldiers never die" in French. He repeated the question a couple of times, slowly, and I think a little incredulously—and then gave me the answer, but somewhat in the manner of a man with doubts about his hearing. He was courteous and helpful, but I'm sure that after he put the phone down he walked away muttering that you sure get some très screwy calls on *this* job—or "Quelle next?"

One more item in the you-too-can-speak-languages department. A friend one day returned from a trip to display across the top of my desk several copies of the cartoons as they appeared in a foreign newspaper—with all the lettering translated—and asked what I thought of the way the cartoons were being used. I remarked with some pride that the paper seemed to be giving them a nice play. Clearly apprised of my ignorance, she then read the cartoons to me. It turned out that the words had nothing to do with the original ideas at all. Whatever the original labels, they were translated to make each cartoon an attack on a native political figure the newspaper hated; and all the titles came out reading something like "How Long Can We Stand This Lousy

"Les Vieux Soldats Nevair Die"

Jun 51

May 51

"Haven't You Heard? The Wolf Was Killed In Korea"

Oct 50

What need we fear who knows it, when none can call our power to account? Yet who would have thought the old man to have had so much blood in him? —*Macbeth*

Apr 51

Government?" The newspaper syndicate explained to this paper in several languages, including the legal, that its renditions would have to be a little more accurate—and after that they were.

The title, incidentally, is a part of the cartoon, and sometimes the most important part. However, some of the magazines and papers that reprint cartoons seem to regard titles as appendages to be altered or chopped off completely. And even a great newspaper which makes a conscientious effort to publish "all the news that's fit to print" sometimes seems to republish cartoon titles and drawings "printed to fit." That ain't fair to the cartoonist, fellows. A cartoon is a one-piece job, and when the drawing or the heading is changed it's not the same cartoon any more. This practice of abridging titles is some day going to prompt me to write a letter to the Edtr of the Nw Yrk *Tms* or the Pblshr of *TM* magzn.

Some cartoons carry no title at all, and the practice of *adding* captions to these is just as bad as removing or cutting those that do belong. The picture of the race to the price-controls deadline recalls a fable that most of us are familiar with. Familiar or not, it's doubtful if anyone would find added meaning in a title, "The Hare and the Tortoise." Along somewhat the same line, I didn't think it necessary to explain that the cartoon of the three little pigs was based on the story of the same name, or that the characters were patterned after Disney's interpretations of these animals. And in a pre-World War II cartoon showing Stalin as "Mona Lisa with a Moustache," there seemed no point in adding a line saying, *After the famous painting, the Mona Lisa, by Leonardo da Vinci*. Or *Thanx, Lennie*.

The title on the Perón cartoon was quite a mouthful. This came about because I recalled a part of the Macbeth quotation, and on looking it up discovered that the preceding sentence was so apt that it had to be included too. But a shorter one wouldn't have done as well.

As for which the cartoonist thinks of first, the picture or the title, I think they usually occur together. Sometimes one or the other might come to mind first, depending on whether the point is mostly visual or mostly in the wording. And this brings us to the question of how cartoon ideas pop up.

For that one I've never had a satisfactory answer, except that they are not what I'd call "inspirational." That is, they come on office time and as a part of a daily routine in which you think about what you're trying to say and draw a number of sketches in an effort to find the best way of saying it in a picture. I can't recall ever suddenly jotting down a cartoon hunch on the back of a score card at the sixteenth tee—or leaping out of bed in the middle of the night to put on paper a picture that has come as if in a vision. It would probably save a lot of time if things worked out that way, although a fellow on a daily job might get a little fidgety wondering when the muse was going to visit him.

"Well, Owen, Things Are Looking Up"

Jun 52

"Do You Think I've Started To Fade, Whitney?"

Jul 52

Anyhow, there's nothing mystic about the business of getting up a swatch of sketches each day and hotfooting it around the office to solicit opinions on them from busy staff members. If you'd care to take a look at the Wastebasket Department, here are some rough sketches:

[UNUSED SKETCHES FOR CARTOONS ON OPPOSITE PAGE]

Above: "Fill The Steins For Dear Old Maine—"
Below: "They Would Have Rallied To Me, Whitney, Rallied To Me!"

Above: Free Ride
Below: "Perhaps If You Put The Magic Hat Back On, Sir . . "

The two sketches of Senator Brewster were among those drawn the day after he was defeated in the 1952 Republican primary in Maine. They were tossed out in favor of the manhole drawing, which is the cartoon that appeared in the paper.

The two MacArthur sketches were among a group done immediately after the 1952 Republican National Convention, on the day when the dressing-room cartoon was selected for the finished drawing.

Ordinarily the defeat or the fading of political figures might not be the best subject for cartoons, but the political careers of these two men had been unusually interesting.

Reactions to cartoons are always interesting, and when newspapers refer to their "alert readers" they aren't just kidding. Readers are sometimes dis-

"... Upset By Radio Commercials On Streetcars? Try Dr. Shmoogle's Soothing Stomach Syrup ..."

Oct 49

"Nobody Can Say I'm Not Working"

May 49

turbingly alert in catching technical errors. Before doing the streetcar cartoon shown here, I had taken a good look at a current-model trolley and at some photographs of Washington streetcars. But a proponent of radio-in-streetcars wrote a long letter-to-the-editor pointing out that my vehicle had no radio antenna on the front, that I showed the motorman holding an old-fashioned hand-switch instead of the levers and buttons used to operate Washington trolleys—and that I had completely left out the underground trolley groove between the tracks which is particularly characteristic of car lines in this city.

Jul 49

Jun 49

All this, of course, had nothing to do with the captive-audience issue which was the point of the cartoon, but from the standpoint of mechanical accuracy the critic had me, all right.

The cartoon of the Senate rowing around in circles was the subject of a running dispute in a contributors' column—the question being whether a boat rowed in this manner would actually move in a circle. Before drawing this one I had tried it out on a colleague more familiar with boats than I, but I hadn't tried it out on the water.

With the aid of mail-order catalogues, newspaper "morgues," and other references, most of us in the cartoon line try to make gadgets look reasonably accurate and workable. But there's no telling what might move a newspaper reader to letter-writing.

As incidental an item as a cat sniffing around a garbage pail, which I've used in a couple of slum drawings, brought me a gentle rebuke from a couple of cat-lovers who had noticed this repetition and who pointed out that cats are not necessarily associated with such unpleasant surroundings. And when I've tossed a crescent moon into a night sky in a drawing some people have even written to say that I've shown the wrong phase of the moon for that particular day of the month.

I don't worry much about irrelevant details like that, and actually the readers don't either. Catching minor items in pictures is a kind of game with some of them, and those Aha-I've-caught-you comments are usually written with a good deal of fun.

The question of what's a good cartoon and what isn't is something that's up to you. I've often heard formulas for what these things ought to be, but I've never heard one that applied in all cases. There are many cartoonists with many styles of drawing; there are humorous cartoons and others that are stark and dramatic—some with many words and some with none. I've seen outstanding examples in all styles; and, along with others in this business, I can only mumble that a good cartoon is a good cartoon. This may sound like Gertrude Stein but it seems to be the only "rule" that fits.

In 1950, the Corcoran Gallery of Art showed a couple of hundred of these cartoons, and *Time* magazine reported that two of the most popular were the one of the elephant on the psychiatrist's couch and the picture of the Taft cat which had just eaten the administration's labor bill, shown on the preceding page. I don't know why these two should have been favorites—or whether the viewers divided along political lines, some sharing Taft's pleasure and others enjoying the G.O.P.'s discomfiture.

When President and Mrs. Truman came to see that show, my feeling of pleasure was somewhat tempered by the thought that there might be awkward moments when we came to cartoons which criticized administration people and policies, or which presented the President in violent caricature. But these were the very cartoons the Trumans seemed to enjoy most.

In a country where the head man can laugh when the cartoon is on him, this really isn't such a bad line of work to be in.

15
Small World

I KEEP SEEING ARTICLES about the scientific possibilities of making journeys that will be literally out of this world; and only the other day I read a straight news story which said casually that on trips to the moon, the first stage—to a space platform—would be made by "conventional rocket." That's what it said in the news story, adjective and all; and it made me feel like crying "Whoa!"—an obsolete word that I picked up as a small boy when the milk and the mail were pulled by horses.

When those jet-finned whoosh-cars start taking off straight up, travelers may have a real opportunity to "get away from it all." But in the meantime it's becoming more and more difficult to get away from anything in this shrinking world. There may be a slight delay before even the "conventional rockets" make regular arrivals and departures, and while we're waiting for the interstellar saucer schedules to come out, here we are stuck on this one-horse planet, problems and all. So we might as well see what's going on.

The cartoons in this section comprise an assortment of 1949–52 drawings which at this writing, with no space-ships in sight, still classify as "foreign affairs" pictures.

The first items we come to are a couple of cartoons on the world financial situation, and that'll give you an idea what a lark we're off on in *this* chapter.

I'm not going to go into all the details and fine points of international exchange here, and for a very good reason. I don't know all those details and fine points, and when money talks in a variety of languages I wish it would speak slowly and distinctly.

During a couple of world monetary conferences here, when the cartoons about the "wampum" and the "three apples" were drawn, my days were brightened by comments from a couple of financial experts who expressed happy surprise that I had read their technical papers on money matters. This was sort of a happy surprise to me too, because I hadn't. But I was certainly glad to know that the fellows who deal with these upper-bracket problems also find those things a little complicated.

As a strictly low-finance guy, what I find easiest to grasp is the fact that some people have more dollars than others. This I can notice without even

"Why Not All Tribes Use-um One Kind Wampum?"

Aug 49

"Wait—Let's Start From The Beginning—
If You Have Four Apples—"

Jul 49

stepping outside the city limits, and it seems to be true the world over—for countries as well as for persons.

If the U.S. were really an individual named Uncle Sam, he might hole up in a town house with all his dollars, or retire to a club to clip coupons for the rest of his life. But despite all the cartoons of the man with the whiskers, there

"This Will Keep Out Competition"

May 52

The Double Whammy

Apr 52

really is no "Uncle Sam." And because we have to trade with the rest of the world, I don't think we're being international Goodtime Charlies or big-hearted suckers when we let the dollars, the imports, and the exports move around. And so I draw cartoons like these about tariffs, an old national issue which has been making quite a comeback lately.

This almost gets us into economics, a subject which is fascinating to economists and which excites most of the rest of us to about the same extent as ¾ gr. of nembutal. What economics needs is a good five-cent word that means the same thing but sounds different.

It's unfortunate that this seems to be a lullaby word, particularly in Congress, where appropriations for world economic programs fail to arouse enthusiasm in a number of legislators.

There's something about a military program that is fine fine fine, and some of our statesmen would distribute arms to any old non-Communist countries as indiscriminately as Crackerjack prizes. The *non*-military programs are important too, but even though they cost much less they generally have harder going up Capitol Hill.

Everybody can visualize an ally (A) pointing gun (B) at enemy (C). A gun goes *bang!* The economic programs that support the arms program just go *chug-chug*. And the technical-assistance programs that help to prevent Communism don't make any noise at all. But they help to win people, who are still the most important items in the world despite all the latest gadgets.

"Couldn't Do Better With A Hammer And Sickle!"

Jul 50

"Don't Be Alarmed. We'll Just Sink the Bottom Part"

Aug 51

I think we need all the people we can get on our side, and in the contest to win them the race is not always to the jet-propelled. To a lot of people, oxcarts are of more immediate importance than rockets, and a good deal less frightening. And it doesn't take a Space Cadet to reach these people and talk to them about plowing.

There have been a number of speeches lately about carrying abroad the Spirit of '76, although there's not always agreement about what's meant by that. Exporting fifes, drums, and copies of the Declaration of Independence—with space to insert name of government—would hardly do the trick, even if we were to throw in loose-leaf copies of our Constitution, with room in the back of the book for adding twenty-two amendments to be sent in later installments. But we can certainly carry abroad a devotion to our own declarations, and show that we mean business about equality and the people's welfare.

We like to hum a few bars of "Yankee Doodle" and think of ourselves as a young country. But as governments go—and they've gone pretty fast in the last century and a half—we're now one of the oldest in the world. We might as well face the fact that some of the younger governments wonder if we're still all aflutter for the ideas we had back in the days when we had just come out of our colonial cocoon. One of the things that makes them wonder about us is the type of policy that sometimes has us stringing along with just the kind of fellows the people of other countries would like to be stringing up.

There's no better example of such a government than the Franco regime

"Why Do I Always Let Him Give Me The Chaperone?"

Jun 50

Ghost Writer

Apr 52

"I Want To Offer To Help You"

Apr 51

"Let Me Know If It Raises Its Head Anywhere"

Aug 51

in Spain, which is a good bet to come off with a prize in any international unpopularity contest. I've had occasion to do cartoons about Franco for too many years now. The caricature rolls easily off the brush, but any time he wants to bow out and make way for a decent government I will not feel bereft.

His features appear in several of these drawings, along with the unshining faces of Tito and Stalin—making a complete assortment of characters not

"The Sovereign Government Of Yugoslavia Is Accused Of Acting Like A Sovereign Government"

Jun 48

"I Too Suffer from Land Hunger, Comrade"

Mar 51

"You Lousy Communist!"

"How's That For A Smart Move?"

Oct 49

Aug 50

likely to be seen together outside of cartoons or maybe an international rogue's gallery.

There are no wings and halos visible on any of these fellows, but when Tito peeled off from the Soviet satellite formation and thumbed his nose at Russian imperialism, this was good news on our side of the iron curtain. And when we sent aid to Tito's Yugoslavia, which is literally under the Russian im-

"Beat It—I Said I Don't Need Any Light"

Aug 51

The Clenched Fist Salute

Sep 49

perialist gun, there was not much room for misunderstanding about what we saw in *him*.

The Let's-Be-Pals-With-Franco drive is something else again. Spain is not under any gun except Franco's, and I'm particularly irked by the efforts of his well-heeled lobby in this country to promote him as a Great Hero.

Quite a few congressmen have plied their way across the ocean to be plied

"I've Shrewdly Managed To Get Him To Join Us"

Aug 50

by this dictator and have come back blowing champagne bubbles about him. Well, from the way they've paid their respects to this fellow you'd think he was Sir Galahad or something—instead of being the lame-duck member of the last previous gang of thugs who tried to take over the world.

The rewriting of history is a pastime on which the Communists have no monopoly, and some of the Reds must be turning envy-green over the job that Franco's lobby has done for him. His press agents have been building him up as the world's greatest champion against Communism, despite the fact that his revolution was begun against an elected non-Communist government and that he "saved" Spain from Communism only after he had first driven Spaniards into the arms of the Communists.

That was back in the Era of Appeasement, which is somewhat painful to remember; so perhaps there is a psychological reason why the Franco lobby has so many takers for its New History.

The last-ditch argument for tying in with Franco is that this is a matter of "military necessity." In a country like Spain where the people are only a little more weary of fighting than they are of conditions under his government, aid to Spain may be a "military necessity" for Franco personally, but I'm not so sure that it is for us. And I don't think it helped to overcome defeatism in Europe when Franco's rooters gave the impression that we were ready to dig in behind the Pyrenees and toss the rest of the continent to the wolves.

The statements about Franco being indispensable to us evidently made quite

"What Would You Charge To Let Me Protect You?" — Jul 51

"It's A Great Privilege To Deal With A Guy Like Me" — Aug 52

"Now To Cut Down On Those Damn Democracies"

Aug 51

"Why Is It That So Many Europeans Turn Communist?"

May 49

an impression on *him,* though. At the end of July 1952, the U.S. State Department got the answer to the question posed a year earlier, when the "What Would You Charge—" cartoon was drawn. Franco demanded (1) an immediate gift of $125,000,000 with no strings attached, (2) large-scale military

"Guess Maybe You Don't Know Who I am, Bud"

Nov 49

"First, Allow Us To Apologize For Our Country's Decadent Democracy And Our Stupid Freedoms"

Oct 49

Mar 51

Mar 49

aid to be provided by the United States, and (3) guarantees which would amount to a United States alliance with his government. Following all this he would then (4) *consider* allowing the U.S. to establish bases in his country. Whether the $125,000,000 was to be delivered in unmarked bills tossed from the window of a moving train or hidden in a hollow tree stump was not disclosed.

Sep 51

Mar 52

"I'm An Old Arab Tentmaker. Slip This On For Size"

Dec 51

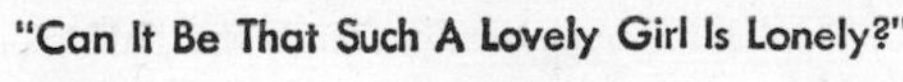
"Can It Be That Such A Lovely Girl Is Lonely?"

Oct 51

Following these demands there was a brief pause for some second thinking about who was going to be doing what for whom or to whom.

The whole "strategy" argument for giving our all for Franco is based on statements by some of our military men who said that—from a strictly military viewpoint—bases in Spain would be desirable. That's a fair enough viewpoint

"What's The Big-Brother Routine Today, Chief?"

Feb 52

"Want To Knock Off Some Communist Allies?"

Oct 49

"Fine! Just Remember To Clench The Fist"

Jun 52

"Look Out—Here Comes Another 'Peace' Demonstration"

May 52

for those military men who hold it. It's their business to figure all the military angles, and we have a civilian government to consider the situation as a whole.

From a strictly military standpoint, a few additional bases anywhere might be desirable, as well as deals with anybody including the penguins at the South Pole.

Member Of The Wedding

May 52

"Well, If It Isn't My Old Pal Again!"

Mar 52

From a strictly military standpoint we could even move in on a few countries if they proved uncooperative. But this wouldn't be advisable, because there are other considerations aside from the strictly military ones. One of these is what the framers of the Declaration of Independence called "a decent respect to the opinions of mankind." This has something to do with strategy too.

And that's what I think is the big trouble with getting unnecessarily chummy with fellows like Franco. It isn't the cost in money or in arms. It's the cost in terms of people who wonder what we stand for in the world. The people of Europe are familiar with the kind of government that Franco represents, thank you. They lived under it during the Axis occupation and they are not exactly frantic for Francisco. They're not likely to be enthusiastic for us either, if we go beating the drums for him and pushing them aside to embrace him.

I've done several cartoons about the similarity between the Communist gang and the old New Order gang of Hitler and Mussolini's day, which putsched people like Franco into power. I think we could make a lot of hay out of that similarity—but not if we get everybody confused by snuggling up to the same kind of characters ourselves.

Well, there are some people who *prefer* to deal with dictatorships, and if you don't mind thumbing back to page 68—a cartoon about that viewpoint appears there under the title "Down Stairway." These people feel that totalitarians make everything simpler and neater. A dictator says he's with us, and that's *that*. No worries about what *people* might do—about what they might think or say, or how they might vote. Everything dandy except that we'd be tossing away all that we're fighting for.

I don't think it's just a funny coincidence that some of the congressmen who are most enthusiastic for dictators are the same ones who are most suspicious of freedom in our country. That kind of mental affliction is difficult to localize. When you get to be afraid of the people abroad, you're likely to be afraid of the people at home too.

Either you believe in the freedom idea or you don't. I think it's great.

16

Home Front

IN A FREE-STYLE MONOLOGUE like this, there's no reason for me to run on tossing off words when I don't have anything much to add to the cartoons, and that's the case with this portfolio of some of the drawings about Korea.

The events which began with the Communist aggression of June 24, 1950, are not easily forgotten, even though some people seem to have mislaid in their memories their own reactions to those early events.

There were some who seemed to think that while the national sword was being sharpened they might as well grind a few axes of their own—and around here you sometimes wondered whether it was a tocsin or a dinner bell that had been sounded. But most of us, including nearly all the members of Congress, were behind the effort, and felt that the action taken by the United States and the United Nations was right and necessary. At the time I thought so too, and I still do.

Here are the cartoons, and I'll be back for the next chapter.

Casualty

Jun 50

"By The Way, Have You Signed Our Petition To Outlaw New Weapons?"

Jul 50

"You Can See How North Korea Was Invaded"

Jun 50

By The Horns

"You Weren't Supposed To Be Able To Hit"

Jun 50

Jul 50

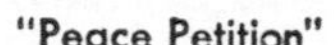

Jul 50

"Fighting Back, Eh? You Dirty Warmongers!"

Jul 50

"Hold It, Fellows. Better Put In Revolving Doors"

Jan 50

"Please Keep The Aisle Clear. You Never Know"

Jul 50

"Germany For Us Germans!—Korea For Us Koreans!—The Philippines For Us Filipinos!—"

Aug 50

"In This Damn Place A Majority Can Veto Us!"

Sep 50

"Those Are The Flags Of Various Gangster Mobs And Millionaires. Now Shut Up"

Aug 50

"Hand Me Some More Of Those Olive Branches"

HERBLOCK

Aug 50

"White Is Black. Black Is White. Night Is Day—"

Jul 50

Interest On A Few Dollars Savings

Jul 50

"Fight Harder! Fight Harder!"

Sep 50

"But First A Few Words From Our Sponsors—"

Feb 51

"Don't You Know There's A War On?"

Apr 51

"Hello—U.N.?—"

Sep 50

"You Know, That Cold War Wasn't So Bad"

Sep 50

Translation From The Chinese

Nov 50

Christmas Shopping

Dec 50

"Five Hundred Million Of Them—All Expendable"

Nov 50

"I'm Doing My Best To Get You In, Pal"

Nov 50

The Burning Fuse

Dec 50

"Aren't You Grateful For All The Strategy I Supply?

May 51

"Oh, Yes—Too Bad—Now, My Next Plan Is—"

Mar 51

"Hear Anything About Where We Volunteer Next?"

Dec 50

"Some Trouble In Some Place Called Korea?"

Feb 52

"Confess! The Americans Sent You!"

Mar 52

"I Want Them Back—They Were My Prisoners First!"

May 52

Dec 51

17

The Asia Game

THIS IS GOING TO BE about Asia from the viewpoint of one who has found some pretty good Chinese restaurants in Washington, and who can remember back to a time when little incense pots were one of the fastest-moving drugs-on-the-market. I just want to let you know at the start that my credentials are right on a par with those of most of the boys who have been spreading their old Chinese laundry checks before Congress, tucking their hands into opposite sleeve ends, and sing-songing, "Asia policy velly bad." This comes to you direct from Formosa-on-the-Potomac, scene of some of the greatest Asiatic battles since Genghis Khan turned in his uniform.

One distinctive feature here is that I have not printed any of the cartoons upside down or turned any opinions inside out to make them read the opposite of what they were originally. This is something of a novelty in the Asia Game, or China policy racket. The Asia Game is the greatest craze to sweep the country since Mah Jongg, which contained only sixteen winds and 144 pieces. This new game is played by looking back over the shoulder till everybody has a pain in the neck, and the purpose is to find out "Who Lost China," which has evidently been misplaced, like a button or a pair of mittens. Any number can participate.

As these cartoons indicate, I think I have a pretty good idea who lost China. My guess is that it was the last person who had China before it slipped down between the gratings. His name is Chiang Kai-shek and however inadequate his leadership of the Chinese people was, he certainly inspired some of the fiercest fighting ever engaged in on American soil.

Every schoolboy knows that if you dig a hole deep enough you will come out in China; and this works in the other direction too. The government of Chiang Kai-shek dug itself into a hole so deep that it came up in the American political scene—or was helped up by loving China Hands.

The drawing of Chiang and the Senate committee is nothing special as a cartoon; but while Congress has been excavating its way back to the Ming dynasty, I dug up this little curio from my own littered nook. It illustrates what was happening in March 1948, when the Eightieth Congress authorized, with some hesitation, a $125,000,000 military-aid program for China. This was part of the more than three billion dollars' worth of aid we extended to Chiang—mostly in outright grants—between 1940 and the autumn of 1951, when we tossed another $400,000,000 into the kitty. More than half of this three billion dollars went to China after World War II. That kind of money ain't litchi nuts; and other governments, more effectively anti-Communist than this one, have done a lot better on a lot less.

I throw this in just as a reminder to busy congressmen who have forgotten that they have had a part in foreign policy, or that we did anything for the Chiang government, and who sometimes seem to feel that nobody *told* them there was such a place as China. There are no cartoons from that period on the subject of U.S. armed intervention in China, and I don't recall hearing much talk about that idea at the time.

The cartoons of Chiang and the Kuomintang government and of Madame Chiang and Uncle Sam were based on the idea that there is a limit to how bad a government can be, and a limit to what we can do for one when its own people are trying to separate themselves from it as fast as possible.

The one of Madame Chiang, like some of the 1951 cartoons of Eva Perón, brought a couple of comments about "bad taste." Caricaturing of women presents some special problems, but I'm a firm advocate of equal rights for political figures in political cartoons; and these gals did not get around just to pick up some new stitches to take back to the home-town sewing circles.

"On Second Thought, You're A Lovely Guy— I Guess"

Mar 48

"As A Last Resort We Could Try Decent Government"

Nov 48

This "Slow Boat to China" cartoon literally struck a popular note because its title was based on Frank Loesser's song of approximately the same name, at that time particularly current. There were a good many favorable comments on it, including one from a scholarly editorial colleague who spends much more time with his books than he does with his radio. A few weeks later he burst in to tell me that this cartoon had reached a pinnacle in popularity. "Do you know what's happened?" he asked earnestly. "Somebody's written a song about it!"

When Chiang went to Formosa at the end of 1949 the Asia Game really got hot. Players of the game could now begin to remember how easily China could have been saved, and could begin to recall exactly what they meant to have said all along. The Game was given an extra boost by McCarthy, quoting China Lobby literature, and it raged in Washington while our forces were fighting in Korea—a place, incidentally, which is also in Asia but which is not the residence of Chiang Kai-shek. By the time the Great Debate on troops to Europe began, in 1951, true Formosa fans viewed Europe as a canasta player might look upon bridge whist.

It seemed to me remarkable that people who had previously regarded the Atlantic and the Pacific as dead-end oceans should now be so fascinated by this particular place. Senators who had shown no great interest in Aid to the Allies, the United Nations, or the Atlantic Pact, and who were cool to the idea of the Eisenhower Army for Europe, were wild about Formosa. It had

"I'd Like To Get You On A Slow Boat To China"

Nov 48

The Great Oriental Disappearing Act

June 51

become the isolationists' Bali Hai and the subject of their Bally Hoo, an enchanted island where anybody who had spent his political life in a closet could suddenly blossom forth as a man of the world.

During this troops-for-Europe debate I drew the cartoon of Uncle Sam being pulled away from Europe by a character labeled "Isolationists," but Editor Herbert Elliston pointed out that technically this did not seem to be

"You Can Still Catch The Boat If You Hurry!"

Jan 50

"Forget About Europe—I'll Take Care Of That"

Dec 50

"Who Does This Eisenhower Think He Is?"

Feb 51

the right word to describe the people that he sometimes referred to as "Formosa Firsters." So I substituted the label "Asialationists." This doesn't do the job exactly because true Asia Game players are really interested only in one particular part of Asia. But at a time when the defense of Europe was almost

"I'll Be Glad When The Great Debate Is Over"

Feb 51

'This Would Be A Perfect Time For You Guys To Shut Up'

Dec 50

going down the Congressional drain, I think it conveyed something of the general idea. There were other kinds of general ideas current at this time, as illustrated by the cartoon of the Napoleon uniform. You could hear the swishing of bullion braid in the oratory.

When former President Hoover spoke of our ocean "moats"—words which suggested the pre-Pearl Harbor notion that "the oceans will protect us"—I

"See Any Knaves Approaching The Moat, Sire?"

Feb 51

HERBLOCK

did the two-worlds cartoon of him and Senator Taft on the little globe girdled by a Hoover collar. Mr. Hoover's collars have gone soft on us lately, but for years he was the political figure who wore no other man's collar, and the outdated high-wall neckpiece seemed an appropriate symbol for his speech.

The Eisenhower Army got in just under the wire. When the MacArthur controversy broke loose, the Asia Game reached a new climax, everybody played chopsticks on the typewriter, and Congress established the Open Mouth policy for China.

May 51

"Do You Have Much Trouble With Him?" | Reveille

Apr 51 | *Apr 51*

The four MacArthur cartoons appeared within a week's time, and others in between were related. The drawing titled "Reveille" was done the day before the MacArthur dismissal. It appeared in the first edition of the Washington *Post* at 9 P.M. the night before, and continued through all editions, even after the 2 A.M. announcement. When I took in the morning paper

"Hurrah For The One On This Side!" | "Wait A Minute, Now—Let's Not Go Hog Wild!"

Apr 51 | *Apr 51*

and saw the headlines about the dismissal it seemed to me that the cartoon was by then outdated. But several people called that morning to comment how timely it was and to ask if I'd had any advance notice on the story. This was pleasant, though in a confusing sort of way. But that was not all. Shortly afterward, a magazine writer took me to task for it, describing it in his article as a rather brutal cartoon done at a time when the President had already made up his mind anyhow. That he had already reached his decision is, I think, obviously true. But in the absence of any pipeline to the Infinite or to the secret counsels of our national leaders, all that most of us can do is to call 'em the way we see 'em and to keep whopping away until something happens. The alternative would be always to assume that "something is going to be done" anyhow—in which case I would be doing cartoons about golf or gardening or something. There must be a lot of good editorial campaigns that have been lost because they were stopped too soon as a result of hot tips that everything was going to be taken care of.

Just to wind this up and make everything completely confusing, the day the "Reveille" cartoon appeared the White House phoned to say that the President would like to have the original drawing. The questions of whether or not this one was timely and whether or not it was rather brutal I will now toss into your lap. Anyhow, that was quite a day, that one.

"I Can Lick Any Man In The House. Carry Me Back In"

May 51

The Tumult And The Shouting Dies;-
The Captains And The Kings Depart

Apr 51

The title of the Marshall-MacArthur square-globe cartoon may be of some interest. In showing sketches to patient staff members that day, I had this one titled "We've Been Using More of a Round One." But two writers commented that the words "Round One" at the end of this line somehow suggested a prize fight. Things were hectic enough without putting Marshall and MacArthur in a cartoon whose title suggested a prize fight even unintentionally. But the real reason for changing it, of course, was to avoid slowing up the

"We've Been Using More Of A Roundish One"

Mar 51

reader. I wrestled with those darn words till deadline time, and finally substituted *roundish* for round. As it turned out, a number of readers seemed to be amused by the word itself.

While the Asia hearings were going on in the Senate, India—another Asiatic country—was waiting for Congress to act on a proposal to send it famine-emergency food. It waited several months and finally received aid on a loan basis after Russia had sent a little grain with a lot of fanfare, and after the

Sermon On The Mount

Apr 51

effectiveness of our action had been pretty well dissipated. The "Sermon on the Mount" cartoon had in it a little extra twist for those who pride themselves on being good Christians but who look with cold superior eyes on our Asian neighbors. One senator made a speech at this time, on the subject of aid to India, in which he recommended what he referred to as an old lawyer's maxim: "Collect while the tears are hot." The tears were hot all right, but this kind of cynical dallying did not set any Asian hearts on fire for us. I thought the grain should have been sent immediately and sent as a gift.

Once more, Christian principles aside, this kind of idealism is also the soundest strategy. Anyone who has any sincere concern about Asia or Asia policy is bound to have a lively interest in our relations with India. But the Asia Game is, as I explained, a backward-looking one. In this game you do not care much about India until good old Chiang Kai-shek moves there or until it is "lost." The cartoon of the congressmen and Point Four illustrates the same type of policy.

By the middle of 1951, Chiang's American fans, evidently more active than his Chinese supporters, had pulled off quite a revolution of their own—not in China of course, but in American policy. The Asia Game had been played so successfully that they were now setting up as the criterion of true Americanism unwavering support for that stanch American patriot, Chiang Kai-shek, who seems to look better from a distance than he did to his own people. Any day now, some senator may spring to his feet to suggest changing the name of the Washington Monument to the Chiang Obelisk.

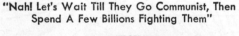

"Nah! Let's Wait Till They Go Communist, Then Spend A Few Billions Fighting Them"

Jul 50

"Do You Swear To Preserve, Protect, And Defend The Government Of Chiang Kai-Shek?"

Jul 51

"Feel Free To Write Whatever You Want"

"We Mustn't Offend Them—They're Very Influential"

Aug 51 *Jul 51*

The cartoons on upholding the interests of Chiang are more a rephrasing than an exaggeration. During 1951 anyone in the Foreign Service who had ever found the Chiang government to be less than perfect—which is to say, anyone who had ever had anything to do with it—was likely to be driven out. And they were damned by people who themselves had expressed the same sentiments. If our reports from abroad are simply going to reflect the opinions of people like McCarthy, we might as well eliminate the Foreign Service entirely and save ourselves some money. The cartoon of the smear bucket tilted over the Foreign Service employe incidentally contains a composite caricature of McCarthy and McCarran.

I don't think the State Department should have caved in to this kind of pressure and propaganda; but it did, and I drew the picture of Acheson and the chopping block. One newspaper reported that a clipping of this one was on Secretary Acheson's table when he walked in to his press conference that morning, that he looked at it and laughed with what the paper called "gallows humor." Mr. Acheson has caught hell from many sides, and it seemed to me that his main trouble was that he evidently regarded fighting as the exclusive province of the Defense Department.

One of the neatest tricks in the Asia Game has been to attempt to destroy confidence in public servants and then oppose them on the grounds that they have lost public confidence. This is one that might cause even a brass Buddha to do a double take, but it's part of the Game. Oddly enough, these fears about loss of confidence do not extend to Chiang, who lost the confidence of his people so completely that they even welcomed the Communists. So much equipment had been handed over to the Communists by his troops—and some of it sold to the Communists by members of his government who put nothing above a fast buck—that a U.S. Central Intelligence Agency officer who had watched a Communist unit move into one Chinese city testified that it was so

"Well, Goodness—We Can't Investigate Everybody!"

completely equipped with American matériel that he thought at first it was a U.S. outfit. Asia Game players asserted that the U.S. helped the Communists, and in a way they're right. The aid we gave Chiang evidently helped to equip a good part of the Communist army.

In all the hustle and bustle to investigate everything connected with China, only a few senators have thought about looking into what happened to the more than three billion dollars we sent Chiang and of investigating what goes with the extremely effective pro-Chiang China Lobby in the U.S. The cartoon of Senator Morse illustrates his efforts in this direction, which are frowned on by true Asia Game players. It's entirely possible that some of Senator Morse's colleagues may soon feel that he has lost the confidence of the people.

For further information and all the latest plays in the Asia Game, watch your daily paper.

James Michener, author of *Tales of the South Pacific* and *The Return to Paradise*, has suggested that it would probably be a good idea if we all cleared from our minds old cliché phrases about the "mysterious Orient" and the "inscrutable East." From this corner of Asia, located between Virginia and Maryland, I'd like to second that. After watching some of the strange moves around here, I think we're lucky if the Asians haven't started referring to us as the "mysterious Occident."

"Now, Here's A General I Have Confidence In"

Feb 52

The Reluctant Dragon-Hunters

Jul 51

18

Strictly Ethical

THERE HAVE BEEN A LOT of highly ethical statements about ethics lately—some of them issued by pious politicians who are so ethical that they have never slugged an old lady to swipe her purse or broken into a church to filch pennies out of a poor box.

Many of these statements contain a few fur-lined phrases about "mink morality"—which refer, of course, to the mink coat as a symbol of unethical conduct in public office, and not to the personal habits of the busy little animals themselves. The number of mink coats actually turned up in Congressional investigations has been few, but the mating of a couple here and a couple there has produced a popular impression that half the people of Washington are in mink up to the eyeballs.

We've all been incensed by the idea of official positions being turned into trading posts, and I've taken my whacks at this sort of thing in many cartoons. But by now there has developed a kind of mink Mumbo-Jumbo which

"Do I Understand There's More Cooking?"

Feb 52

"I Can Protect Myself From My Enemies—"

Oct 51

makes so much of obvious symbols that it can't recognize unethical conduct unless there's a furrier's label sewed in the collar. I think the ethics problem is a little bigger than this. There's more than one costume for corruption. The field of political immorality can't be covered by a few pelts, and I don't think we ought to let anybody pull the fur over our eyes.

Most of the fur that's been flying lately has been in the form of dead cats

Bipartisan Slum

Mar 51

aimed at the executive department, and some of this barrage has certainly been deserved.

As early as the beginning of 1946 there was occasion for cartoons like the one of the filling station, on the nomination of Oilman and Democratic Party Fund-raiser Ed Pauley to be Undersecretary of the Navy. Mr. Pauley's name was withdrawn when confirmation seemed impossible. But it was the fight over this nomination that resulted in the abrupt departure of Secretary Harold Ickes from the Truman cabinet. This seemed to me to be a bad swap on anybody's team, and I think it set the pattern for some of the Truman administration's troubles that came later. One of these troubles was a shortage of pitchers who could toss a first-class thunderbolt when the occasion required.

In fairness to that administration, it might be mentioned that all the outside operators who claimed "influence" with the government actually did not have it. And a government official can hardly be blamed because racketeers prey on suckers with stories of how palsy-walsy they are with him. But there was enough influence and there were enough favors in places like the R.F.C. to make people wrinkle their noses; and when the Internal Revenue cases broke, the smell of corruption was unmistakable.

Among the drawings on those cases is "The Little Fixes That Spoil the Vines," which required an all-night editorial guard to beat back attempts at "correction" by proofreaders who know their Biblical quotations.

The extent of the corruption may have been exaggerated, but it was there,

"He Polished Up That Handle So Carefullee That Now He Is the Ruler of the Queen's Navee"

Jan 46

"Come Back Any Time"

Mar 51

The Little Fixes That Spoil The Vines

Oct 51

Internal Revenue Collection

Dec 51

the cleanup was too long delayed, and the great rhubarb between Attorney General McGrath and Investigator Newbold Morris inspired no confidence in the administration's ability to handle a broom in its own house.

Much of the unethical conduct in the executive department struck me as being downright cheap—a mediocre kind of political immorality of mediocre

Apr 52

New Broomstick

Apr 52

"But Still In Matters Vegetable, Animal, And Mineral, I Am The Very Model Of A Modern Major-General"

Sep 49

"When Are You Going To Plug It In?"

Jan 52

men—and that's what made it so hot politically. Its very cheapness, involving deep freezes, wholesale coats, and free hotel rooms, made it easy for everyone to grasp—easier than big-time political immorality, which involves higher

When The Pie Was Opened The Birds Began To Sing

Mar 51

"Yeah, But It's Pretty Hot Back Home, Too"

May 52

"Who's The Suspicious-Looking Character Over There?"

Jun 51

"What's Wrong? We're Doing This In Broad Daylight"

Jun 51

mathematics and is difficult to visualize. Everyone can picture a mink coat. But things like padded contracts, special tax exemptions, and excessive subsidies seem rather remote. And figures running into hundreds of millions of dollars are just more big numbers. They aren't photogenic.

If a fellow is going to go in for unethical conduct, he's obviously better off to be big about it and stay away from the almost-familiar items. A coat or a car worth a few thousand dollars is a thing some so-and-so has that the rest of us haven't been able to get. But a million dollars is on a higher plane. And a billion is up there in the stratosphere.

The really big "influence cases" which reach those upper levels are in the influence of special interests on the U.S. Congress. The kind of political immorality that sacrifices the public interest is not necessarily illegal, but it's a lot more costly to the country than the sell-out of some public official for a few bucks.

In its report on ethical standards in the federal government, the Douglas Committee, in 1951, neatly summed up the situation by quoting an old English quatrain:

> The law locks up both man and woman
> Who steals the goose from off the common,
> But lets the greater felon loose
> Who steals the common from the goose.

Congressmen who would not steal a goose from any village common would yank the rug from under the consumers of natural gas, or pull out from under the federal domain the resources of an ocean floor.

During the 1952 debate over offshore resources, the Senate admitted a couple of lobbyists to the floor of that chamber. It seemed only fitting. Perhaps it would be a good idea if lobbyists regularly appeared on the floor with

"Mink Is For Peasants"

Mar 51

some of the senators and were identified for the gallery spectators. You can't tell the players without a scorecard.

The "tidelands" quitclaim bills were legal in the sense that Congress could vote them. If it wished, Congress might also vote to give away the Washington Monument and Fort Knox. Maybe I shouldn't even suggest the idea.

The money lost to consumer-taxpayers through gimmicks in the "controls" bills and special-interest loopholes in tax bills would buy mink for plenty of us. But you can't see these sums—or drape them over your wife's shoulders.

Incidentally, the accepted term "loopholes" is perhaps a misleading word to describe these exemptions. It sounds as if the special interests profited through some involuntary oversights in the drafting of these measures. The loopholes are not accidental. They are bored by representatives and senators who know what they're doing.

These are some of the big-money items. Congressmen who do their best for the special interests assert that such bills involve only differences of opinion about the public welfare. But there have also been more homey types of questionable ethics in the legislative branch, going all the way down the scale to payroll kickbacks, for which a couple of congressmen have been convicted.

In recent years, Congress has given more and more time to investigations, sometimes to the neglect of its regular work. The Eighty-second Congress (1951–52) broke all records for inquiries by conducting more than 230 of them, including many which involved waste of time and money. It has grilled private citizens and government officials. It has probed the present and the

"Just Big Enough To Drive A Few Trucks Through"

Sep 51

"I Think I'll Investigate Hollywood's Morals"

Mar 50

past. But Congress has not done much investigating of itself, and in several cartoons I've tried to hint that it might be overlooking a little gold mine right on its own Capitol Hill. It evidently feels that this kind of digging, so close to home, might be boring—not to say painful.

A quick check of Congressional payrolls—conducted by a newspaper—has revealed a surprising number of surnames identical with those of congressmen. There's nothing wrong with relatives of legislators receiving government pay-

"If There's Anything I Hate It's Sloppy Neighbors"

Dec 51

checks if they are earning them, as many undoubtedly are. Just how many is something that only Congress can find out. Other departments have been investigated for less. And the roster of congressmen engaging in nepotism includes some who are among the loudest in denouncing bureaucratic boondogglers and the first to demand staff cuts in other parts of the government.

There are a number of other interesting matters of ethics which Congress can consider without doing any probing outside its own offices.

When a senator or representative accepts free plane rides from airlines interested in legislation, he is traveling far above the agency official who occupies a free hotel room. But I don't think he'd register any higher altitude on a morals meter.

When a too lively interest in legal business or other enterprises brings private interests into conflict with the public interest, this is no better for congressmen than for administrators. And it's not been unheard-of for legislators, as well as other public servants, to dabble in commodities, stocks, or real estate while in a position to affect price fluctuations or to be in the know on coming developments.

Congressional reluctance to put the heat on itself has been most apparent in its investigation of others. Some of the testimony in the "influence" and tax cases strongly suggested that congressmen themselves had sometimes exerted questionable influence. This has produced some embarrassing mo-

"Oh, Pretty Good—How Are Things With You?"

Jun 50

"Anybody Care About Influence On Me?"

Oct 51

ments during which Congress has had to look for a pencil it mislaid or has suddenly remembered an appointment with the dentist.

Neither house of Congress has adopted any of the codes of ethics proposed for congressmen or for Congressional committees, and some of the investigative-committee abuses involve their own forms of political immorality. But where congressmen have questioned their own colleagues they have been the very models of courtesy and graciousness.

The King Subcommittee, investigating Internal Revenue cases, found it necessary to invite Senators Owen Brewster and Styles Bridges to testify about their connections with "fixer" Henry Grunewald—later cited by the House of Representatives for contempt. The deference shown them was in considerable contrast to the treatment given many other citizens and distinguished members of the government who have appeared before Congressional committees even on routine business.

There was no bullying or relentless probing of the senators. Senator Brewster's explanations of the checks that passed between him and Grunewald were a little difficult for many people to follow. But if the committee was confused it was evidently too polite to display its confusion before a senator.

When Senator Bridges of New Hampshire was asked about his intervention, at Mr. Grunewald's request, in the seven-million-dollar tax case of a liquor dealer in Maryland, he explained that he regarded an interest in such matters as a public duty. There are no territorial limits on the devotion of a senator to public duty, and there is no evidence that the senator was motivated by anything less than his sense of duty. But one could not escape the impression that if he had explained his actions by saying that it had been too cold to play badminton at the time, the committee might have been equally satisfied, equally delighted, equally grateful for the explanation. Why, of course! How charming! So nice of you to have come!

Congressmen do have a certain code of ethics, even though it sometimes seems to be rather an exclusive one.

Congressional interest in the Big Cleanup cooled somewhat when President Truman proposed that Internal Revenue collectors be Civil Service instead of patronage appointees. This one passed with 37 nays against it. But when the President further proposed that United States marshals, postmasters and customs officials also be brought under Civil Service, the bellow from Capitol Hill was something like that of a wounded bull. The senators voted down this reform by almost 2 to 1.

Another Presidential proposal provided that sources of all outside incomes of upper-bracket members of the government—including senators and representatives—should be made public. There's room for argument about this

"Well, A Fellow Can't Spend All His Time Hunting"

Jan 52

"What's Going On Down There Among The Mortals?"

Apr 52

one, but some of those outside incomes are certainly of interest from an ethical standpoint.

In the cartoon of the boy athlete and the moneybags, drawn at the time of the college basketball scandals, one of the moneybags refers to the $35,000

"What Do You Figure This One Would Cost?"

Sep 50

"How Could You Kids Lose Your Sense Of Values?"

Mar 51

annual salary paid to Senator Bridges as a trustee of the United Mine Workers Fund, while also serving as a U.S. Senator at $15,000 a year. Another refers to the $10,000 paid to Senator McCarthy by the Lustron Corporation for writing a small pamphlet on housing; Senator McCarthy was a member of a Senate committee dealing with housing.

Congressional campaign funds also figure in that cartoon, as they do in the one of the Senate chairs. Some of the gentlemen occupying those chairs have shown less than a wild enthusiasm for thorough investigations of campaign contributions. And there were no hurrahs for the 1950 House committee investigating lobbying when it significantly suggested that a joint committee be set up to check on laws governing operations of lobbies and the conduct of elections "because of the close relation between the two." Such a committee was never established.

When the Senate Elections Committee investigated the 1950 Ohio senatorial election, Senator Taft guessed that expenditures on his behalf might have run as high as $700,000. Other observers have figured the amount spent to have been over $2,000,000. We'll probably never know all the statistics on that election because it turned out that the treasurer of Mr. Taft's campaign had a carefree method of receiving and disbursing funds which did not involve tedious bookkeeping. The investigating committee did not press him beyond the point of human endurance.

At this writing, Congress has not yet passed a bill providing that all cam-

Non-Composite Campaign Picture

Mar 51

"Going To Call On Him For A Post-Election Speech?"

Nov 50

paign funds shall be accounted for and made public.

A little matter of ethics was involved in the 1950 senatorial campaign which elected Senator John Butler of Maryland. It was in this campaign that the faked photo of Senator Tydings and Earl Browder was used, and the "non-composite picture" cartoon was drawn when the Senate later investigated this election. The Senate deplored some of the campaign techniques but allowed Mr. Butler to keep his seat.

Senator Butler and then-Republican National Chairman Guy Gabrielson professed to see little difference between a composite photo and a cartoon.

There is a difference, and I can tell them what it is. It's the same difference that exists between a counterfeit bill and a picture of a moneybag. The latter represents the idea of money but it doesn't try to pass as currency. A cartoon presents itself as a caricature, a pictorial exaggeration, the expression of an idea, signed by the creator of that idea. It's accepted exactly for what it is, and it isn't trying to fool anybody. I don't think people like Senator Butler of Mr. Gabrielson should try to fool anybody either, not even themselves.

The word "corruption" generally brings up a mental picture of somebody pressing a few bills into somebody else's hand. That type may lend itself best to cartoons, but it's not the most common form. Any time a public official in the performance of his duties puts anything ahead of the public interest, that's in some way a form of corruption.

It's not necessary for money to change hands directly or even indirectly.

Sep 51 *Apr 51*

The desire to gain office or to keep it can be as corrupting as a bag full of bills. It's possible for a politician to be bought and paid for without personally receiving a nickel—or a fur coat. The office or the hope of office can be quite enough. And there have been congressmen originally elected in campaigns against predatory interests who were later re-elected with the aid of those same interests.

The campaign contribution, the favor, the job that's given during or after a term of office—whenever any of these things is given "for services rendered" in office, that's a payoff and not much different from any other kind of payoff.

It's sometimes said that a party long in power tends to become corrupt—although, oddly enough, a glance at history seems to show that the major scandals occurred when an administration or a party had not been long in power. It may also be that a party long out of office tends to become irresponsible. That's a form of corruption too, and a dangerous one. But corruption is too personal a matter to be hung on Father Time; and I don't think parties must necessarily be corrupted by terms in or out of office.

Fear and Smear, reckless charges, the abuse of privilege and authority, are politically immoral—and corrupting in a way that can't be measured in money at all because they corrode basic values.

For a person to be worthy of public office there must be some things he won't do and won't tolerate to get it. From the earliest days of this country we have had public figures who spoke up for the rights of political minorities to express unpopular opinions—and who felt that basic American principles were more important than their own political fortunes. But we haven't seen enough of this kind of political morality lately, when some aspirants for the highest offices have been happy to encourage the idea that any who disagree with them must be traitors. Political morality consists of something more than raising the arms heavenward and being able to say, "Look, Ma—no hands in the till."

Nothing exceeds like excess. It's probably easy for a politician to assure himself that his party or faction must win, to go on from there to the premise that he must be The Man, and finally to take for granted that anything is justified if it helps him to win: "Anything goes," "It's all politics," "Don't be naïve."

Anything does not go. We have a right to expect the best from our political system, and if we want democratic government to show its worth we've got to demand the best from it. The end doesn't justify the means in domestic politics any more than in international politics. The late Henry L. Stimson said that "the only deadly sin I know is cynicism." And I think we ought to be naïve enough to holler murder whenever politicians try to get away with murder.

Well, as I started out to say, there's been a lot of talk about this ethics stuff lately and about the need for a cleanup. I'm all for that—for ending corruption in all its phases and in all branches of the government. But I don't think we're going to get that great moral revival just by cleaning out a few grafters who are corrupt in the more obvious ways, or by crying tallyho at a mink.

Not all the skeletons in all the political closets are wearing fur coats.

Mar 51

Oct 50

19

Something New All the Time

ONCE WHEN I NEEDED to get a couple of weeks off, the newspaper syndicate that distributes the cartoons simply reissued some old drawings. It explained that these were done in previous years, but spared the subscribers that old line, "Reprinted by request." And the subscribers were evidently so taken with the novelty of this presentation that none of them complained.

One of the newspapers that received this batch of cartoons hit on the even more novel idea of running all of them as a group, accompanied by an editorial which said in effect: These cartoons on current national problems were first published about three years ago, and it's a sad commentary that they're still appropriate today.

There are no actuarial tables on the life expectancy of cartoons, but people

"I Never Catch Up!"

Sep 51

"Want To Meet My Friend Too?"

Jan 50

"Great Age We Live In, If We Live" — *Aug 50*

"We'll Be Counting On You For Volume 7" — *Dec 51*

who make a hobby of collecting editorial drawings occasionally express a preference for "something that will always be good." They feel that art is long and time is fleeting, or at least that this is the way things ought to be. One cartoon collector told me that he had been wanting to ask for one of my drawings but was waiting to find one that would never get out of date. Then, while we both stared at the floor in mutual embarrassment, he coughed slightly

Ol' Man Congress, He Jes' Keeps Rollin' Along — *May 47*

"Wait! Let's Think It Over Another Thirty Years" — *Jan 52*

and added that he hadn't yet seen any of mine like that. I'm afraid he's not likely to, and as a matter of fact I hope he doesn't.

Writers have remarked that pieces written to be good for all time usually turn out not to be very good for any time. In any case, the cartoons are drawn for right now. There are plenty of subjects for comment these days. Posterity can do its own drawing and writing about its own problems, and we may be

"Anything Your Little Heart Desires"

Jun 46

"It Sure Is"

Jul 49

"Don't Go To Any Bother - - -
I'd Rather Just Drop In."

Oct 50

doing all right if we can just see that they don't have to do their drawing and writing on the walls of caves.

When the cartoons are about things that I think need improvement, they can't get out of date too quickly to suit me; and there have been times when I've been happy to toss away unused drawings because of some unexpected happy turn of events. Unfortunately, a lot of the cartoons don't get out of date, because the problems they depict keep hanging around or keep repeating themselves. It's something new all the time, but often about the same old things.

I don't mean such certainties as death and taxes—or the weather, which would be an unlikely subject even if we could do something about it. Weather cartoons, in fact, are extremely hazardous, and nothing is so outdated as a cartoon about a long dry spell which appears on a day when the subscriber has to fish his newspaper out of a flooded yard. The cartoon of the melting Capitol was done during one of Washington's more intense heat waves, when the weather succeeded in dominating everything else around here. I figured I couldn't lose on that one because it would be worth the loss of a day's work if the cartoon would perversely produce a cool breeze—but it didn't. There was obviously no hope of climate control through cartoons. The next day I bought an air conditioner.

Most of the subjects already covered in these pages have been recurring themes. The headlines change, some of the faces change, the names on Congressional bills change, but many of the issues remain the same. Congressional

"Big, Ain't It?"

Jan 49

"I Said I'd Cut The Grass Come Hell Or High Water"

Mar 47

investigations multiply and poke into new fields, but attempts to decide what's fit for us to see and hear on television are not a great deal different from attempts to decide what we should be allowed to get through such old-fashioned media as radio and the movies.

There have probably always been cries of outrage from Congress about federal spending—and ever since the Constitution was established, it has been

"Hey! What's Idea Waste S'Much Money On Bread!"

May 50

"I Said, 'I Hear You're Coming Down!' "

Jan 47

"I Thought Your Friend Couldn't Stay Long"

Mar 47

"Tut Tut—Drive On"

Apr 47

Congress that has controlled the purse strings and that has appropriated every penny of the money for that federal spending.

I've assembled here a few cartoons on inflation and controls dating from 1946 to 1952. Except possibly for a brief period in 1949 when there was some talk that we ought to shift fears, go into reverse, and worry about *de*flation, the general problem has remained pretty much the same.

"Get Down—It's Not Over Yet"

Feb 48

"It Sure Ain't Santa Claus"

Nov 50

"Up, Up, Up And Away!"

Jun 47

"Where Did Everybody Go?"

May 51

The "meat producers' strike" of 1951 was reminiscent of the "great meat shortage of 1946. From year to year Congressional hearings on controls featured much the same kind of pro-and-con testimony, with a few interesting variations. In 1951, a congressman told a witness for a consumer group that the legislators were not receiving as many letters in favor of effective price

No Shortage Of This Livestock

"Up!"

Sep 46

Jun 51

"Where Do I Come In?" — *May 49*

"Don't Worry—I Might Catch You" — *Nov 51*

controls as they had received at the time of O.P.A. The witness replied that hadn't done them much good. During the same period, the annual cartoons on rent controls comprised a kind of serial like *The Perils of Pauline*. Each year as these controls were about to expire, Mr. Public hung by his fingernails. Each year Mr. Public grew weaker—and so did the controls.

"998—999—1000—Here I Come, Ready Or Not" — *Jan 51*

"They Went Thataway" — *Jan 51*

"That's About The Size Of It"

May 52

"Nothing's Out Of Control. We Designed It That Way"

Dec 51

Inflation and controls don't last forever. As an economist of the grocery-store—or how-much-did-you-say-that-costs?—variety, I'm not acquainted with all the charts and statistics. But I think it's pretty well agreed that when an inflationary boom gets out of hand, it's followed by a dull, depressing thud. If that happens, I will be sure to get a letter from somebody saying, "You and

"Let's Come To Order, Class. The Next Shift Is Waiting"

Apr 50

"Think This Crop Is Worth Saving?"

Sep 49

your cartoons about inflation! *Now* look what we've got. I hope you're satisfied!"

There's one perennial problem that I want particularly to note, and that's the school situation. I've mentioned before that a cartoon on almost any subject is likely to get a reaction from somebody. But the response to the school cartoons has been on an entirely different scale from most of the others. Requests for reprints of these come in regularly and from all parts of the country—not only from established organizations but from citizens' groups in small towns where they think of education in terms of a bond issue for one new school building or of one new schoolroom for their kids.

This interest is no tribute to the cartoons. It's simply an indication of the screaming need for more and better schools across the country. Any cartoonist who wants to get in a few licks on this subject will find a large audience eager for stuff that can be used in national or local campaigns to dramatize the need.

Perhaps "dramatize" isn't the right word. There isn't much dramatizing to be done. The children aren't actually coming through holes in the roof, but they *are* jammed into obsolete and inadequate buildings that are all but coming apart at the seams. With many schools operating on two or three shifts a day, the children are receiving "part-time education" in overcrowded classes. And so many classes are being held in locker rooms, boiler rooms, storage rooms, warehouses, and other unlikely places that public education in many parts of the country is almost beginning to look like an underground movement.

"See What We Mean?"

U.S. SCHOOL SITUATION

CONGRESS

May 50

"It's Too Small To Play House. Let's Play School"

Oct 50

In April 1952, Earl James McGrath, U.S. Commissioner of Education, appeared before a Congressional committee to read a statement based on the nationwide school-facilities survey which had been authorized by Congress. This report is quite educational in itself.

On the basis of twenty-five representative states which had already taken part in it, the survey showed that only one-fourth of the school buildings can

The Bent Twigs

HERBLOCK
©1949 THE WASHINGTON POST CO.

Sep 49

be rated as "satisfactory," and even among these "satisfactory or fairly satisfactory school plants," 61 per cent of the classrooms are overcrowded.

Everything is overcrowded except the teachers' pay envelopes. There seems to be a shortage of money for teachers as well as for schools, and consequently there is getting to be more of a shortage of teachers, too. This means still more students per class and still less education for them. What with low pay, difficult working conditions, and general harassment, schoolteaching is not a very attractive occupation these days.

Perhaps the reason teachers are regarded with so much suspicion by some of our Nervous Nellies and professional Know-Nothings is that it's hard for these people to believe that teachers would take such a beating without having some sinister purpose.

Aside from the fact that the kids of this generation are losing out on education, the present school facilities don't even give them a break on safety standards. The old gags about small-fry hoping the schoolhouse will burn down aren't so funny any more in view of the fact that many of the school buildings today are firetraps.

Commissioner McGrath reports that "of the total children enrolled, one in every five is in a building clearly not meeting minimum fire safety conditions, and an almost equal number are housed in buildings the safety of which is doubtful." He goes on to cite a safety survey which shows that "over a 15-year period there has been an average of more than 2100 schoolhouse fires per year.

"Well, Here We Are Back In School, Sort-Of"

Sep 50

"Gee—Each Of 'Em Has A Whole Seat To Himself"

Oct 49

In 31 of the more disastrous of these fires, 395 persons suffocated or burned to death."

Perhaps we shouldn't worry about the children's minds at all. In some of these firetraps maybe they're lucky just to get out with their skins.

When a band swings into the strains of "School Days," a lot of people with nostalgia-for-places-they've-never-been practically dissolve in sentiment for the good old Little Red Schoolhouse. Well, they can dry their eyes now. It turns out that "two out of five school plants now in use have only one room." While these one-room jobs are occupied by only 6 per cent of the school children, they're overcrowded too, and even more inadequate than they used to be.

Of course school children today are no longer "taught to the tune of a hickory stick." There probably wouldn't be room to use a stick anyhow, without whopping four kids by mistake on the backswing. And if the children still carry slates anywhere except in cartoons, they may not have elbowroom to write, "I love you, Joe." They probably just scrawl, HELP!

There never seems to be a good time for providing better school facilities. In the 1930's we had that depression, and school construction dropped off. After the depression there was the war, and *that* was no time for building schools. Then came the post-war period, inflation, rearmament and everything. For more than twenty years now it's evidently always been a bad time to build schools.

Maybe there's never a good time for better schools—unless we think that schoolhouses are as important as garages, hotels, and amusement places. Maybe there's never a good time for education—until we decide that the future of this country has a priority, that the next generation of Americans is important, and that the time to build schools is whenever they're needed.

Meanwhile the children keep coming along, and more of them than ever. The bumper baby crops of World War II are now jammed into the elementary schools, and—are they getting that big already?—in a few more years they'll be crowding the high schools. And here's an item in the paper that says the population of the U.S. is over 156,000,000 now. It was only a little while ago that the population had just reached 150,000,000, wasn't it?

The Office of Education estimates that 600,000 new classrooms and their supplementary facilities must be provided by 1957–58 if the unprecedented demand for school construction is to be met.

The birth rate "has gone up ever since 1936," Commissioner McGrath told the Congressmen, "and is currently higher than ever before in our history. . . . There is no indication that the number of births will fall. Hence, we cannot delay building schools in the hope that there will be fewer children.

Moreover the new millions of additional children must get their educational opportunity *now* as they grow up, or they will not get it at all."

It's something new all the time—including new kids in school buildings that are older, more cramped, more dilapidated than ever.

"I'm In The Fourth Grade, Third Shift, Second Layer"

Sep 51'

20

And in Conclusion—

WHEN THE PROGRAM COMMITTEE of a club gets desperate enough, it will try anything. So the secretary of a local outfit phoned one day to ask me to give a talk on "The Use of the Arts in Propaganda." We both went through the usual pleasant protests; and I was sufficiently flattered by being asked to speak on a subject of this scope that my arm had to be twisted only up to the elbow.

There followed a couple of weeks of searching books and newspaper files to dig out information, badgering friends who had been with the O.W.I., and lying down on a couch at intervals to probe my subconscious for items going back to the posters of World War I.

When the time to speak arrived, I relayed all this hard-won information to the club members, going on for about forty minutes to recite the number of surrenders in Korea as a result of leaflets dropped over enemy lines, and the percentage of British printing-plant capacity devoted to underground activities in occupied Europe during World War II.

At the conclusion of this effort the chairman asked for questions. There was a flat silence which was finally broken when one of the members rose to say, kindly but frankly, "That was a very nice talk, but you didn't tell us anything of what we wanted to hear about. What we wanted to know is, what's it like to do a cartoon every day?"

I was not stunned for more than a minute, and with true *savoir-faire* managed to say "Huh?" and scratch my head without tipping over the water pitcher. Under pressure I might concede that my stuff is some form of art, and I suppose anyone who expresses a viewpoint is a propagandist of some sort. But it seemed to me that the assigned title was a good deal oversized for a talk about the daily job. Anyhow, we went on to have a nice, informal discussion and everything came out all right.

Maybe *you've* been waiting to hear something about the daily schedule, too. When the Washington *Post* put out a special issue on the dedication of its new building, all of us in the various departments were tapped for pieces about our particular tasks. This extra chore came at kind of a bad time, but there was nothing compulsory about doing it. You were perfectly free to let it go, and nobody would think any the worse of you except that you'd just be a complete heel and a disgrace to the institution, that's all. The result was the following account of *How a Cartoon Gets Drawn.* On reading it over I find that it contains a couple of slight exaggerations, but let it go:

* * *

The assignment to do a piece on "How a Cartoon Gets Drawn" couldn't have fallen into more willing hands, because the subject is one that I often wonder about even if nobody else does.

Let us try to figure out here just what happens to those golden hours between the morning arrival, when you stride briskly to your drawing board whistling off-key, and the close of day, when the porters cart your limp form down the hall with the waste paper and help you press the elevator button.

You first read the morning mail, beginning with the card from Schmurtz, Schmurtz, and Schmurtz—none of whom you know—announcing that their law firm is being joined by a Mr. Schmurtz. You continue through the letters asking why you haven't answered previous letters; and on down to the anonymous postcards saying (a) *Why don't you drop dead and give the proletariat a break, you capitalistic snake!* and (b) *So you are rapping McCarthy again; well, you will be laughing out of the other side of your face when we take over, you snake!*

There is a final note which does not descend to political bickering but merely says with simple dignity, "Yu stinck."

You are now off to a happy start and proceed with the reading of the morning paper. As you go through this and a couple of out-of-town papers, you jot down down possible cartoon subjects on a note pad which you will later try to decipher. There comes then the time to go over these notes and settle back to give those subjects a good think.

It is at this point that the door opens slightly and a visitor asks if you are busy. You say, Yes, you are, and he says, "Ha! It looks like it!" and sits down for a long chat. He is followed by three others who open with the same conversational gambit.

A cartoonist who keeps handy some wet mortar and a supply of bricks can lay a few rows of masonry while he is being reflective, and thus give visible evidence that he is working. But the disadvantage of this device is that he may concentrate so intently that he will end up by walling himself in, and miss his deadline completely.

As the visitors leave, the phone rings and a voice asks if you ever use suggestions for cartoons. You say, No, you are sorry but you don't. And the voice says, "Okay, here it is: You draw a picture of a rat, see? And label it Stalin. Get it? A rat, see?—" When you have thanked him and hung up, you find that a small delegation of ladies has come in to ask if you can't do something about our feathered friends who, it seems, are multiplying faster than the number of statues on which they can perch.

The ladies are followed by a colleague who pulls out snapshots of himself, his wife, his mother-in-law, and his six kids and wants caricatures of them all together and he knows it won't take you long.

You are now well behind your theoretical schedule for the day and it is high time you drew up some sketches and submitted them to Editor Herbert Elliston. He will select one of these for the next morning's cartoon. You will then do it over in ink and take this completed drawing to the engravers who, according to the mystic rites of their craft, will all look at the clock and chant in unison, "Where-the-hell-you-been-up-to-now?" With a series of secret incantations which cannot be printed here, they will then photograph your drawing onto a metal plate which *can* be printed. It is this plate, or "cut," wrought by enchantment out of zinc, which will magically disappear on the way to the composing room just before press time.

But to get back to that drawing:

You are almost ready to start on some sketches when a former friend who is now selling insurance walks in. While he is taking off his hat, coat, and shoes, he tells you that he just dropped by to say Hello. He then bares his teeth in a grim smile and draws from his briefcase a twenty-page outline of an endowment policy designed especially for you. He also remarks that you're not looking well, which at this point is undoubtedly true. You finally make a deal that if he will leave immediately you will provide him with a lifetime annuity and pay him double indemnity in case he should develop paralysis anywhere outside your office.

As the deadline draws nearer, the word gets out that you are pressed for time and the phone rings more frequently. These calls include a couple from people who have swell ideas for cartoons. Listen, you draw a picture of a rat, see? And label it Stalin!

There is also a call from the *Buttonhole Manufacturers' Monthly Journal,* which wants to reprint a cartoon that appeared in 1946 or '47 and they don't remember the title, but will you send over a copy right away? You are very sorry, you can't right now. At this the voice becomes insistent and tells you that they *must* have it right now because they are making a *deadline*.

When a telephone has been torn loose from the wall socket so that only a few thin shreds of wire remain, it is best not to try to fix it yourself. A simple call to the phone company—over a different telephone, of course—will bring

a repair man. He will ask you how it happened and you can explain to him that the phone must have fallen out the window.

You are about ready to start on those sketches and let's get going. There now enters an acquaintance who wants an old drawing but he does not wish to disturb you. "You just keep on working," he tells you; and, quiet as a mouse, so as not to disturb you, he takes all of your drawings out of the cabinet, spreads them over every inch of floor space, and walks back and forth across them on tippy-toe, leaving hardly any heel prints on them at all. He selects one that you wanted to keep, asks you to sign it to him with the modest inscription, *"To good old John, the greatest guy in the world,"* and departs. But not without first looking back over the havoc he has wrought and commenting that you sure keep a messy office.

It is an invariable rule that all visitors who tear apart your files must comment that your office is untidy; and all callers who sit on your desk for half an hour must remark that you really ought to organize your time better. This is in accordance with an Act of Congress.

The next arrivals are a reader who agrees with your cartoon in this morning's paper, a reader who disagrees with it, and a semi-pro baseball team who did not see this morning's cartoon but just dropped in to practice short bunts.

You are now ready to start on those sketches. That is, just as soon as you have talked with this visitor who says that his friends tell him he looks like Herbert Hoover, and would you like him to pose for you? For a slight extra fee he will also bring in a live elephant that he has tethered to the outer doorknob.

Elliston's secretary stops by to say that the editor is getting ready to leave and if you want to show him sketches you'd better make it fast, bud. You are still ready to draw them when there appears a man leading six full-grown mastiffs that he wants to give away. He is looking for the columnist who runs items about pets, but he will settle for you. While you are trying to talk above the baying of the dogs, the phone, which is once more in perfect working order, starts ringing again.

And it is at this moment that there arrives as a mixed group a committee for the revival of the Whig Party, four unidentified boys who set to work making paper cutouts of your cartoons, a fellow who wants to know where is the gents' room, two window washers with pails, and the complete original cast of the *Student Prince*.

You are now ready to . . .

* * *

The article ended there. I suppose it might have wound up, "You are now ready to try doing a book."

That's where we came in.